# Utah: The Complete Ski & Snowboard Guide

# UTAH
## *The Complete Ski & Snowboard Guide*

**Includes Alpine, Nordic, and Telemark Skiing & Other Winter Sports**

Michael R. Fine

The Countryman Press
Woodstock, Vermont

FOR MY DAD, WHO INSPIRED AND ENCOURAGED
MY LIFELONG PASSION FOR SKIING.

ISBN 978-0-88150-742-3

Cover photo © 2008 James Kay
Interior photos by the author unless otherwise specified
Book design and composition by Hespenheide Design

Published by The Countryman Press, P.O. Box 748, Woodstock, Vermont 05091

Distributed by W. W. Norton & Company, Inc., 500 Fifth Ave., New York, NY 10110

Printed in China

10 9 8 7 6 5 4 3 2 1

# Acknowledgments

When I told people I was writing a book on skiing and snowboarding all 13 of Utah's resorts, the sarcasm was rampant. People would comment on how difficult it will be to explore the beauty and terrain that make up these amazing places. They remarked how hard it was going to be and that they had a lot of pity for me. Well, their sarcasm aside, it was a demanding book to bring together and couldn't have been done without a lot of people.

During the two months of assembling the material for this book, I was separated from my beautiful wife, Tricia, and my ski buddies, Elizabeth and Emma. My family was relocated to France and the hardest thing about working on this was being separated from them. It was tremendously brave and generous for my mother-in-law, Carolyn, to offer to come to France and play nanny to my children. I love her and appreciate her support.

Thank you to Greg Tanner and Troy Jaskowski. These two friends accompanied me on many of my visits and helped by taking photos, reminding me of things to note, and generally being there to make the most of my trips. Their help was huge and I do appreciate it. Also, thanks to my dad for hopping on a plane and coming for a visit. It was the highlight of my adventure.

Unlike other ski destinations, Utah's resorts are less competitive and more collaborative. They work together as a team to help send a message. Utah is a great place to ski and you really ought to visit! Each resort is different and has a distinctive appeal. In my pursuit to capture this appeal, I had a lot of help. Each destination had one or more people helping me achieve my goals. All of them were supportive, generous, and friendly.

Here and now, I want to thank all the people individually who took time from their day to show me their mountain. Every host expressed their passion for their resort and why people should visit. I appreciate their enthusiasm and I hope the text here conveys the information and the enthusiasm they provided. The following are presented in the order I visited.

*At Sundance, thanks to Valene Hulme, Lucy Ridolphi, and two other hosts who helped me explore their resort. Thanks to Tim Rencher and Kathy Cavaliere for teaching me the art of pottery. It was a great experience.*

*At Park City, thank you to Bill Battersby and Ian Patrick for showing me every corner of the resort and to Paula Fabel for making it happen.*

*Thanks to Tyler Jackson and Connie Marshall of Alta. Both of you were wonderful hosts and I appreciate your generosity.*

*At Snowbird, Laura Schaffer skis way too fast but she knows the resort. Thank you to her and to Julia Partain for their kind and generous help.*

*Thank you to Andy Cantor at The Canyons for the great day and thank you to Libby Dowd for arranging it all.*

*Deer Valley exceeded all expectations . . . as usual. Jennifer Lewis was a delight and Amy Erickson was an amazing host. Thank you to both of them and to Erin Grady and Emily Summers for arranging all the details.*

*Brian Head has a great ambassador in Bob Whitelaw. Thanks for all your help.*

*At Powder Mountain, my sincere thanks belongs to Paul DeLong and Marc Paulsen. It was a magnificent day.*

*Beaver Mountain has a legend working in their midst. Thanks to Wendell Liechty for the great coffee, cookie, and time. Also thank you Marge Seeholzer for arranging the day.*

*Solitude has a great team in Nick Como and Jay Burke. Thank you so much for the incredible day hiking.*

*Brighton shared two of their best with me along with some deep powder. Thank you so much, Randy Doyle and Rob Cary.*

*Wolf Mountain gave me a lot of great help. Thank you so much, Barbara McConvill, Terri Murphy, and Cindy Beger.*

*Mary Rowland at Snowbasin was always there if I needed anything. Thanks for everything.*

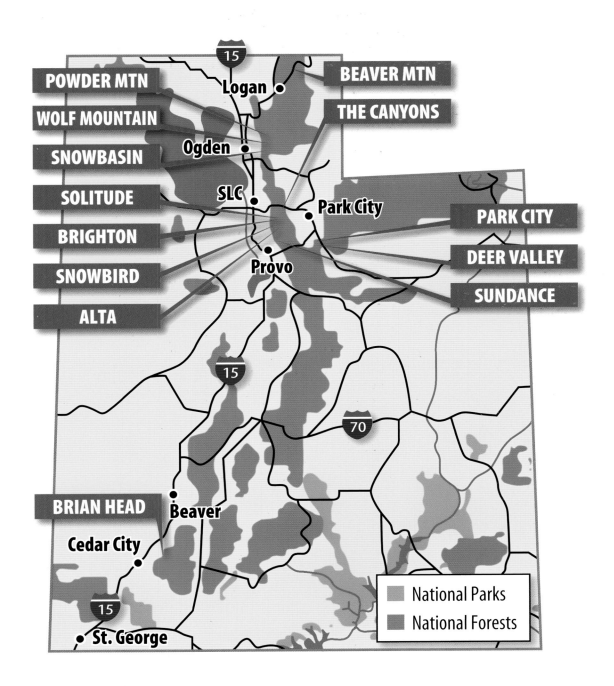

POWDER MTN

WOLF MOUNTAIN

SNOWBASIN

SOLITUDE

BRIGHTON

SNOWBIRD

ALTA

BEAVER MTN

THE CANYONS

PARK CITY

DEER VALLEY

SUNDANCE

BRIAN HEAD

Logan

Ogden

SLC

Park City

Provo

Beaver

Cedar City

St. George

National Parks

National Forests

# Contents

**Introduction: Utah and the Greatest Snow on Earth  1**

*Utah's Connected Resorts*  2

*Utah Myths Debunked*  3

*Resort Amenities*  5

*Mountain Sports*  9

*Prepare for Your Visit*  12

*Common Sense*  15

*Rating the Slopes*  19

*Saving Some Bucks*  23

*Using this Book*  25

**1** Alta Mountain Resort  29

**2** Beaver Mountain  41

**3** Brian Head Resort  53

**4** Brighton Resort  65

**5** The Canyons  79

**6** Deer Valley Resort  93

**7** Park City Mountain Resort  107

**8** Powder Mountain Resort  121

**9** Snowbasin Resort  133

**10** Snowbird Resort  147

**11** Solitude Mountain Resort  161

**12** Sundance Ski Resort  173

**13** Wolf Mountain Resort  185

**Glossary  195**

# Introduction: Utah and the Greatest Snow on Earth

There is an old urban myth that claims that the Inuit people of Canada and Alaska have hundreds of words for snow. In fact, they have as many descriptions as there are in English. Regardless, there is one word in their language that describes Utah's snow perfectly and it is quvianaqtuvik. This is their word for heaven.

Prior to experiencing my first Utah winter 20 years ago, I was somewhat skeptical of the boastful license plates that stated the greatest snow on earth. I wondered how different could it be. I had skied in the Midwest, the East, and much of the Colorado Rockies. It seemed to me that this was merely a marketing gimmick to attract tourists.

However, this is no gimmick. Simply stated, Utah has the most amazing snow I have ever experienced. I am not certain how it happens, but I have heard numerous suggestions. Some hypothesize that the Great Salt Lake has something to do with it, while others note that it might be the high desert or attribute it to our unique location on the globe.

Whatever magic happens is simply unimportant. The end result is a variety of snow unique to Utah. It almost defies description. It is soft, white, and strangely dry. When the powder is deep, it feels like carving turns through a cloud. Supple, smooth, and delightfully effortless, Utah's powder suspends you and gently carries you down the mountain.

When the powder is packed, it forms itself into a silky and gentle surface that lends itself perfectly to turns. Like soft butter icing, packed Utah powder lightly glides across the surface of the landscape

BRIGHTON RESORT

▲ Cutting first tracks in powder in Utah.

can plan on good conditions most of the season. And if you are fortunate enough to visit during one of the frequent winter storms, you are in for an amazing and very special experience.

## Utah's Connected Resorts

When a person plans a ski or snowboarding vacation, they often consider a single destination resort where they will spend the entirety of their visit. However, what if you could take a vacation and have virtually a dozen resorts to choose from and all of them a short distance away? Welcome to Utah.

Utah is unique for many reasons. Besides the amazing snow, breathtaking mountains, and wonderful hospitality, it also has remarkable convenience. All but one of the 13 resorts in the state are located within two hours from the airport, and 11 of the resorts are within an hour and 4 are a mere 40 minutes away.

A visitor could feasibly land at Salt Lake City International Airport in the morning and be on the snow enjoying his or her vacation by lunch. Experience Alta's powder, take a gondola ride up at Snowbasin, or hit the half-pipe at Brighton all after grabbing your gear at the baggage claim. Utah is exceptionally convenient.

One of the best things visitors note is the quick access to the resorts. Unlike other destinations, Utah's mountains are very reachable. The state has an excellent infrastructure to get you up to the resort fast and easy. Most resorts are only a short canyon drive from a major interstate highway. All have bus access, and parking is usually very good.

Another benefit of their close proximity is the connection between the resorts. You can easily visit one resort in the morning, and with

covering the slopes flawlessly. The snow provides the perfect substance for navigating turns.

Of course, the conditions on a warm spring day can be wetter than most of the year and certainly cold days can get a little icy. However, these are rare instances. You only a short drive, spend an afternoon some-place else. Some of Utah's areas even are phys-ically connected. You can buy a pass to ski two resorts and enjoy both in the same day.

Utah's mountains are not only connected together through the Wasatch Front, they are connected through a collaborative effort to encourage everyone to visit the state. Rather than be completely competitive, they recog-nize the huge advantage Utah has with the variety of offerings in a short distance. Many will actually take you to another resort through a shuttle or other service.

You will not only find each resort to be hospitable and unique but discover they encourage people to visit other areas. While each retains a certain pride about their ter-rain, they also recognize that each spot has something different to offer. From the luxu-riant Deer Valley to the quaint Beaver Mountain, each destination in the state is a single facet of the diamond that is Utah.

## Utah Myths Debunked

There are a lot of myths about skiing and snowboarding in Utah that have prevented people from making it their choice for a win-ter vacation. Some of these myths do have a small basis in truth, while others are outright false. Regardless, the following information should clear the mountain air.

### You Can't Get a Drink in Utah

Not only can you drink alcohol in Utah, you can do it seven days a week and the laws are fairly liberal. Alcohol is served in most restaurants and you can usually find a few good bars in any town. There are a few dif-ferent rules, but these are easy to understand and certainly don't impede your ability to have a drink.

▼ Utah offers cosmopolitan dining and excellent variety.

SNOWBIRD RESORT

Beer, wine coolers, hard lemonade, and similar products are sold in grocery stores, convenience stores, or gas stations every day and everywhere. In most parts of the state, these items can be purchased at any time, but a few counties do restrict sales on Sunday morning.

If you want hard liquor or wine, they are sold at state-owned stores. These stores have a relatively good selection and operate at normal business hours. In most cases, you can purchase from 10 AM to 10 PM Monday through Saturday. However, in smaller areas, the stores may only be open until 7 PM.

Many restaurants in Utah have beer and wine lists and some even have full bars. It is simply a matter of choice. Each restaurant is different, and whether or not they serve alcohol is up to them. Most ski resorts have alcohol available and the neighboring restaurants usually offer it as well.

Bars in Utah are not hard to find, but the rules are slightly different than what you might expect. In Utah, a bar is called a private club. These bars require a membership to enter. Memberships are usually offered for two weeks or annually. However, as strange as this appears, it is actually quite easy.

Think of the membership as a one-time cover charge. You fill out a small card and pay a few bucks and you can use the bar as often as you like. The membership card does need to be brought with you into the club, but you can bring up to seven friends along.

Utah also has taverns, brew pubs, beer bars, and lounges that all sell beer and some sell alcohol. These places have no membership requirement, and in some of our brew pubs, you can find nationally recognized, award-winning beers.

The only hitch in all of this is the kids. No one under 21 can enter the premises of a bar, tavern, beer bar, or lounge. Children are welcome in restaurants and you can drink while they are there. However, if you plan on going to a private club for an evening of cocktails, the kids have to stay home.

Also, be smart and do not drink and drive. Utah has some of the stiffest penalties in the nation for DUI offenders. At .08, you are in violation and you can expect to lose your car, lose your license, and spend a lot of time in jail. Bars, restaurants, and other business have numbers for cab services.

In all, drinking in Utah is very accessible. If you are looking to enjoy some après ski or you simply want a cocktail with dinner, you will find Utah just as hospitable and enjoyable as any other resort in the nation.

## Everyone is a Mormon

The Church of Jesus Christ of Latter Day Saints (LDS) makes its home in Salt Lake City. Settling the region more than 150 years ago, their influence can be felt not only in Utah but throughout the American West. However, this is a real benefit to Utah and its visitors.

The Mormons are friendly, tolerant, and welcoming people. Many spend the early part of their adulthood on what are called missions, where they leave home for a year or more to tell people of their faith and encourage membership. As a result, they have had an opportunity to experience other cultures, learn other languages, and meet new people.

Mormons are clean living. This means they don't smoke or drink caffeine or alcohol. However, just because they choose this lifestyle, it does not mean they expect others to live this way. In fact, you can find a Starbucks or a great local coffee shop anywhere in Utah, and as noted previously, a drink is easy to find.

In 2002, the Olympics were held in Salt Lake City and the world was shown that Utah is a hospitable place with friendly people. More than 20,000 volunteered to prove that the world is welcome here. Today, that hospitality remains and Mormons and non-Mormons alike encourage visitors to come to Utah.

The demographics have changed significantly over the years with the influx of out-of-staters, so LDS members are becoming outnumbered in the Salt Lake and Park City areas. However, it makes no difference. As a group, the Mormons are kind, friendly, and a significant part of what makes Utah a wonderful place to visit.

## Utah Resorts Are Outdated

There has been a strange misconception that Utah is behind the times. People seem to think that our skiing and snowboarding is mostly for locals. There is a belief that our resorts are small and that our mountains do not offer the challenges of some of the bigger resorts in other states. This is complete nonsense.

Annually, many Utah resorts are usually in the top 10 in most ski magazine reviews. They achieve this distinction because they are at the forefront of the ski and snowboard industries. Things like gondolas, trams, and high-speed detachable chairs can be found at most of Utah's resorts.

Some of the largest resorts in North America can be found in Utah. In fact, the single largest resort in the United States is Powder Mountain, with over 5,500 skiable acres. What is even more amazing is you can access 11 of Utah's 13 resorts within an hour drive of one another.

However, if your favorite aspects of a winter vacation are endless drives, long lift lines, high prices, and crowded accommodations, perhaps you may want to consider another destination. Utah resorts focus on giving you the most skiing and snowboarding, the best service, and the greatest snow on earth.

## Utah Is All About Meat and Potatoes

There is no question that you can find some pretty spectacular steakhouses in Utah. Throughout the state, a good steak is the pride point of many restaurants. However, there are also some amazing sushi bars, noodle parlors, or French cafés. Simply stated, Utah has a cosmopolitan selection of world-class restaurants.

The last 20 years has seen growth in the amount and variety of restaurants in Utah. Every flavor of cuisine is offered. Local restaurants explore international fare as much as the local color. You can find wonderful and delicious Indian food within miles of a great Mexican place. Utah has it all.

## Resort Amenities

Each resort strives to provide different features for their guests. However, there are some features that most, if not all, resorts will offer. Because these features are common, I have not included them as part of the general resort information.

### Host Programs

A host program is a collection of people put in place to help make visitors feel welcome. Most programs use hosts to provide tours, give directions, or assist resort guests with

▲ Kids will have fun, learn, and improve their skills.

simple issues. These people wear resort coats that help identify them from other skiers and snowboarders. They often have designated spots on the mountain where you can seek them out.

Host programs have been instituted around Utah at different resorts over the last several years to much acclaim. With their success, other resorts have begun implementing programs and now most resorts have some sort of program in place. Some, like Deer Valley, are extensive and offer many different services. Some are smaller and simply place people in key positions to answer questions.

## ☺ Tips and Tricks

Many resorts start host guided tours at the base around 10 AM and 1 PM. If you want to get more comfortable with the resort and where to ski, these free tours are a great way to start. If there is not a free tour, ask around and you might find a host to volunteer.

Be certain to seek out a host. These employees are usually locals who have a love for the resort and like to spend their spare time working to help guests have a good experience at their resort. They have developed an expertise about where to ski and will have insider knowledge. If you are visiting alone, a host is a nice companion for an afternoon. They also give the latest information about things going on in the area and at the resort.

## Ski and Snowboard Schools

Every resort in Utah has a ski and snowboard school and every one of them is excellent. As simple as it is, resorts only benefit when someone comes, learns, and leaves happy. Thus, each resort invests a significant amount of money into their ski school program to ensure it meets the needs of all their guests.

A lot of Utah resorts have strong programs targeted for kids. In fact, many resorts now incorporate a package with child care, ski or snowboard lessons, and a day at the resort. You drop the kids off in the morning and pick them up at the end of the day. At that time, your child will have new found confidence on their board or skis and have a smiling face from all the fun.

There is also a new found emphasis on helping adults learn. There are women's clinics, powder clinics, bump clinics, and tons of other opportunities for you to learn, improve, and grow in your chosen sport. Take up telemarking or get some training on how to ride the rails. These programs are not just for beginners.

## Ski Patrols

Utah resorts have some of the best patrols in the world. This combination of volunteers and professionals is out on the mountain to ensure everyone has a safe and good time.

▲ The ski patrol plays an important part in your safety and fun.

Their role is not simply one of assistance, they are also the watchdogs. They are looking out for you and everyone at the resort and can be a valuable resource. Of course, the cross on their jackets indicates medical assistance, but they can and do provide much more.

## ☺ Tips and Tricks

Unfortunately, ski patrol uniforms are not the same at every resort. While red-and-white is a generally accepted color scheme, it is not necessarily what they will be wearing. When you first arrive at a resort, make yourself familiar with its ski patrol uniform. Though it is unlikely, you never know if you might have to flag down someone for some help.

If you have issues with anything, you can always rely upon the ski patrol to assist. If you get lost, hurt, cold, or just confused, the patrol will help make certain you get what you need. If you find yourself too wet or too cold and can't make it back to a lodge, many mountains have patrol huts around the resort where you can get warmed up.

## Rentals

Every resort has a rental shop and they usually match the size of the resort—the larger the resort, the larger the shop, which means more options. On a basic level, all resorts provide skis, snowboards, boots, and poles. In some cases, you may be able to rent helmets and other accessories. The bigger resorts have a larger variety of choices including different ski and snowboard types and better equipment.

There are a few things you should know before you rent. First, no matter how fast you think it might be, it is going to take some time. There are forms, there is fitting, and there are other people. The whole process will take at least 30 minutes and possibly longer. Thus, you ought to plan ahead by getting to the shop early or renting the day before. Nobody wants to be excited to ski only to be held up with rentals.

Come prepared. You will need to know your weight, height, shoe size, and ability. Vanity has no place in a rental shop. Your safety is at risk here. Ski bindings are set based upon these factors. Whether or not a binding releases when you fall is based upon the accuracy of this information.

Last, rentals will require a credit card and someone over 18 years of age to sign the form. If you know you are going to be using them for a longer time, be certain to tell the shop. There are often discounts available for multiday rentals. In addition,

▲ Essentials or souvenirs, resort shops offer it all.

they need to know when you plan on returning the equipment.

## ☺ Tips and Tricks

Better equipment doesn't really make you better. If you are a beginner, there is no reason to spend a lot on demos or fancier equipment. A basic package is designed to help you have a good day on the slopes and serve your basic needs. As you improve and become more advanced, the better equipment does make a difference and you may want to experiment.

## Ski and Snowboard Shops

Most resorts have their own shop for equipment, accessories, and winter sports fashions. These shops usually have a good selection of the basics but are usually very pricey. If you forget your gloves or need a new hat, plan on paying a premium when you buy at the resort. However, you may find something unique that is branded, which will make a good souvenir.

## ☺ Tips and Tricks

If you forget something like a pair of gloves or a hat, you may not need to buy a replacement. Rather, check the rental shop or the resort information desk to see if they have spares. Many times, there is a lost-and-found and things have been sitting for a while. It is not the most hygienic thing, but it may be a better option than spending a bundle on a replacement.

Deals can often be found on the slopes. These shops offer large discounts at the end of the season, and if you are visiting in the spring, it may be a good time to pick up some nice equipment at a cut-rate price. Many resorts close down for the winter, and as such, want to clean out their inventory for the following year. By the time spring rolls around, they are eager to make room for the new models.

However, don't expect reductions on things like souvenirs. They don't change that much from year to year.

## Parking

One of the worst parts of visiting a resort is the parking. You are directed by people to the corner of a lot where you have to listen to others blast their stereos while you put on your gear. Then you have to haul your equipment through a lot packed with cars in boots designed poorly for walking. Finally, once you arrive at the lodge, someone has inevitably forgotten something important and back to the car you go.

There is an easier way. First, if you have a big group, you can sometimes drive up close to the front of the resort at a drop-off point. People who aren't driving can get ready on your way up the hill, and then when you get to the resort, they hop out and the driver changes at the car. There is no need for the passengers to buckle up boots. Just make certain they have everything before leaving the car.

Watch the parking lots for shuttles. Often, resorts will provide a bus or cart that goes around picking up visitors. If you don't see a shuttle, you may want to start walking to the resort because it may take a long time to make a loop around the parking lot or it may not be running.

## Mountain Sports

### Alpine Skiing

One of the older variations of winter sport activities, alpine or *downhill* skiing can be dated back hundreds of years. However, it was not until the late 19th century that it

BRIGHTON RESORT

▲ Utah's deep powder is perfect for any mountain sport you choose.

started to gain popularity. In Utah, resorts started experimenting with it as a winter recreation opportunity in the 1930s. Today, it is one of the most popular sports in the world.

Alpine skiers use two separate boards, each with an inside and outside metal edge. Large plastic boots are attached to the ski via a mechanism called a binding. This keeps the legs, feet, and skis attached to the boards. The skier uses poles for rhythm, for balance, and to occasionally push forward.

Skiing has made significant advances in technology and skis now come in numerous varieties—fat skis for powder, shaped skis for advanced turning, twin tips for hot dogging, or long skis for racing. All these types only slightly resemble some of the original skis that people used. These changes have improved the sport in terms of safety, ease of use, and overall enjoyment.

People can take skis anywhere on a mountain and have relatively good balance, buoyancy, and speed. The current designs permit skiers to float in deep snow and carve on the surface of packed snow. This flexibility has opened up unlimited terrain and possibilities for the sport, which continues to expand its appeal and popularity.

Utah has a strong commitment to skiing. Many ski industry businesses have their operations headquarter in the state. Utah dedicates millions of dollars annually to promote skiing as a tourism draw. Even Utah's license plates wear the moniker THE GREATEST SNOW ON EARTH.

## Snowboarding

Snowboarding is a close cousin to surfing and skateboarding. Riders position themselves near the center of a long board and strap in. They use a front and back *side* edge to carve turns and control speed. Snowboarding is completely different from skiing in its movement, stance, and operation. Skiers can't simply hop on a snowboard and start using it any more than a snowboarder can start skiing.

Snowboarding is often considered a relatively young sport, but in fact, it can trace its roots back to the 1960s with the invention of the Snurfer. However, in the last 20 years, the sport has really come into its own. What

was once a sport of rebels has now moved into the mainstream. Professional competition in snowboarding is worldwide and part of the Olympics.

Today, you will see as many snowboarders at a resort as skiers. The sport is exceptionally popular with people starting in mountain sports. In fact, in 2006, 60 percent of all new equipment purchases were snowboards. However, in Utah there are still two resorts that do not allow the sport. Deer Valley and Alta have both decided to keep snowboarding out (read their resort profile for more detailed information).

The remaining 11 Utah resorts that do support snowboarding do so with tremendous fervor. Many create custom terrain parks, half-pipes, benches, and other amenities for snowboarders. Marketing and advertising dollars feature both snowboarding and skiers. They have embraced both skiing and snowboarding as part of their clientele.

## Nordic Skiing

The grandfather of winter sports, Nordic or cross-country skiing is an activity in which the participants wear long thin skis with boots that have an unattached heel. The primary design of the ski is to allow a walking motion so that the rider has the ability to trek across flat landscape while still effectively skiing downhill.

Nordic skiing used to be a method of transportation in Scandinavian countries hundreds of years ago. Today it is used as a way for people to commune with nature. People who Nordic ski spend their time getting exercise and enjoying something similar to a walk in the woods.

Many resorts in Utah offer trails for cross-country skiers to explore. Often these locations are very close to the slopes and are professionally groomed to ensure easy gliding. The settings are peaceful, pristine, and designed to help people relax.

## Telemarking

In olden days, it was called three pinning to define the boots used with their unique three pin bindings. Now it is the ballet of mountain skiing. Telemarking incorporates a hiking-type boot and detached heel binding of cross-country skiing with a traditional downhill ski. This unique mixture allows its rider to gracefully sweep down the mountain with bent knee turns.

Telemarking is not an exceptionally well-known or popular version of skiing, but it has seen an increased interest. On a day at a Utah resort, you may see a dozen people on *tellys*. However, many people who are focused on backcountry skiing have found the sport perfectly suited to their needs. The flexibility of the free heel allows them to reduce the amount of hiking.

RENAE BUNKER

▲ Telemark skiing combines Alpine and Nordic technologies.

### ☺ Tips and Tricks

Many resorts rent telemark equipment and those who try the sport find it to be a refreshing and more relaxed approach to downhill skiing. In addition to being a lot of fun, the skills acquired in telemarking help with skiing in rougher terrain. However, the sport is much more physically taxing. New enthusiasts need to be prepared to work out.

## Ski Blades

Taking a page from the book of snowboarding and a page from the book of skiing, the newest entry into the winter sports category is ski blades. Closer to the size of a pair of ice skates, ski blades look like miniature skis and use the same skills. However, because of their exceptionally small size, they provide the freestyle nature of snowboarding.

Ski blades are slowly growing in popularity. Skiers wanting the thrills and exhilaration of snowboarding but not wanting the learning curve and expense are adopting the sport. The exceptional freedom created by the small size of the ski blades gives the rider a chance to perform tricks, play on terrain park features, and experience many of snowboarding's biggest attractions.

# Prepare for Your Visit

The preparations for a winter vacation in Utah involve more than packing clothes and grabbing your gear. The different climate and the complexities of the sports present unique challenges to ensure you have a safe but fun time. It is important to be properly prepared for a variety of situations. From the unpredictable nature of the weather to the physical impact of skiing and snowboarding, you need to be ready for what *might* happen.

Often, the excitement of a vacation can make some forget important basics. Things like goggles or gloves seem small, but without them, you can receive serious injury. Before you head out the door, consider the following potential issues and be prepared with the proper gear and mental attitude.

## Altitude Sickness

One of the amazing things about the mountains of the Wasatch Front is how they seemingly pop up from the earth. In most mountainous regions, there are foothills and lengthy drives to get into the higher elevations. However, in Utah you can be in the mountains in less than 30 minutes after arriving at the airport.

While it may be tempting to jump on the lift and take a fast ride for the beautiful views, it makes more sense to take it slow and get yourself acclimated. Altitude sickness is a real issue for some visitors and it is incredibly important to make certain you take the time to get your lungs acclimated.

## ☺ Tips and Tricks

Hydration is very important at higher altitudes. Carry a small bottle of water with you while you enjoy the mountains. The water will be refreshing and it will help you adjust to the altitude quicker and easier.

## ☺ Tips and Tricks

Moving from sea level to above 6,500 feet (2,000 meters) can cause nausea, vomiting, headaches, and other physical problems. The thinner air in the mountains can be very hard to adjust to if you are not used to it. The best way to adjust is to simply take it easy. Allow your body to adjust to less oxygen. In addition, keep yourself hydrated. Drink a lot of extra water and soon you will feel like one of the natives.

Getting acclimated is different for everyone. Some people adjust much quicker than others. If you feel weak or are getting a headache, slow down and let your body get some oxygen. If you want to ski or snowboard on your first day, just take it easier. Don't attack the mountain. Rather, take some cruisers and enjoy the mountain at a slower pace.

## Sun

Back when I was in high school, the *raccoon* look was a mark of pride. A darkly tanned face minus the spot where goggles or sunglasses were worn was proof of a mountain ski vacation. Times have changed and we now understand the damage the sun does to our skin and are smart enough to take proper precautions.

Sunscreen is not usually something people consider during the winter months. However, when you are at high altitudes, good protection is even more important. In addition, the reflective properties of snow can contribute to the intensity and potential damage of the sun. Even though you may not have a lot of exposed skin, you still need to keep it properly covered with a strong sun screen.

## Eyewear

In addition to the damage to your skin, the brightness of the snow and sun can be very damaging to your eyes. It is also important to remember that light plays a significant part of winter sports. It is constantly changing and good quality eyewear can make the difference in your safety and enjoyment on the mountain.

High-quality eye protection is an absolute necessity on the mountain. You will need something with 100 percent UV protection and a lens coloring that helps improve your visual acuity on the slopes. You may also want to invest in polarized lenses. These will help eliminate the glare from bright snow and give you better visibility when conditions are sunny.

Some people prefer goggles while others like sunglasses. The simple fact is that these are two completely different kinds of eyewear and serve different purposes. Goggles will provide the best all-around use. They protect you from wind, give a good field of vision, and offer the same protective properties as other eyewear.

Sunglasses are more popular with the fashion-conscious. They can provide a better field of vision and are better for people who need corrective lenses. In addition, they are often more comfortable, portable, and easier to manage. Sunglasses do not have to be expensive to be effective. They just need to protect you from the sun.

Eyewear is critical because light plays games on a mountain slope. During the winter months, the light changes often. From bright sunny days to gray and overcast, the weather impacts how we see things all around us. Unfortunately, the changing light

▲ Protective eyewear is essential to enjoying your day on the slopes.

RENAE BUNKER

and its effect on the snow is significant and can be very dangerous.

Because snow is white, we need a nice bit of sunshine to highlight its features. The shadows created by the sunlight help us identify cuts, bumps, and the properties of the snow. However, if the light becomes *flat*, then the terrain turns into a featureless white mess.

Flat light is a very real and consistent problem in winter sports. Whenever it snows or the sky takes on a pall color, we lose our ability to discern bumps, ice, holes, and other surface features. As such, what you could easily anticipate and maneuver around suddenly becomes hidden in plain sight.

Good eyewear can intensify shadows and give you improved vision. Everyone should invest in at least one pair of goggles designed for flat lighting conditions. Typically, a rose lens is ideal for this kind of weather. If you night ski, yellow is good for the electric lighting. Yet, new technologies are always coming. The key is to have the right eyewear for the right conditions.

## Temperatures

Winter in Utah is very strange. Often we will see large storms pummel our mountains, while in the valley it is simply raining. If the snow does stick, it usually does not stay for more than a day or two. The important thing to remember is that as you ascend, the conditions become harsher. Mountain temperatures are not the same as valley temperatures.

Temperatures at the resorts are much colder than in Utah's valleys. The mountains get more wind and more cloud cover, and the increase in altitude matches a decrease in temperatures. In most cases, you should plan for cold. Utah does occasionally have a weather phenomenon called an inversion, where the mountains are nicer than the valley. However, temperatures on top are still much colder.

## ☺ Tips and Tricks

The most effective method of dressing for skiing or snowboarding is to put on multiple layers. The layers of clothing capture air and warmth and keep you comfortable throughout the day. In addition, it is easy to shed a layer if you get too warm or add one if you get cold.

For example, you might wear long underwear, sweat pants, and ski pants on the bottom. Then put on long underwear, a T-shirt, sweater, and jacket on the top. Glove liners, a nice hat, and good ski or snowboard socks are a good investment as well. If your feet or hands feel cold, your whole body feels cold.

## Exhaustion

Skiing and snowboarding are challenging sports that use muscles most of us ignore

RENAE BUNKER

▲ A bright sun doesn't always mean a warm day, so be prepared.

most of the year. When we first get on the slopes, the adrenaline and excitement of being in the mountains make us want to do as much as we possibly can. However, by the end of the day, our bodies become exhausted and we put ourselves in danger.

When you get tired, you risk injury. Our bodies are slower to react, and in skiing and snowboarding, reaction can make the difference between stopping and crashing. If you find yourself getting tired and your body aching, take a rest. A small snack and a short break in the lodge may be all you need to get your energy back.

If you continue to drag and feel like you can't effectively control your equipment, it is time to quit. Even if it's earlier than you planned, your safety is critical. Exhaustion is not something to treat lightly. People get stranded on mountains because they are physically unable to get down. Know your limits and respect them.

## Common Sense

This book is all about the resorts of Utah and how to make the most of them. I have gone to great effort to ensure that all the data is accurate and the material is clear. I want to provide you with the best information possible for making the most of your vacation. Yet, even with the best information, your first obligation is to use common sense.

Skiing and snowboarding are fun and exciting sports when done safely and in control. The following information contains things to consider when taking to the slopes. Everyone wants to get the most from their visit to Utah. Just remember that your safety and the safety of others need to be top priorities to enjoy the day on the mountain.

### Weather Conditions

Mountain weather conditions can change in a moment. You can go from sunny skies to pounding snowstorms in a matter of hours, and it is incredibly important to take the time to prepare. Preparation is not simply listening to a weather report, but it involves having the right gear for the right conditions.

For starters, make certain you bring a pair of goggles even on a sunny day. Sunglasses certainly look cool, but in windy, snowy, or flat light conditions, they are not as effective. Goggles with the proper lens color provide better range of view and are less likely to fog because they sit farther from your face.

Next, make certain to dress warm and in layers. If the temperatures warm up, you can always shed clothing. However, if it gets colder you may end up ruining your day. In addition, you may want to consider picking up some of the disposable hand warmers. They work great and get the blood flowing back to frozen fingers.

Last, if you are bringing your own gear to the mountains, make certain it is properly tuned. Poorly tuned skis and snowboards become dangerous in icy or slushy conditions. They lose responsiveness and can cause injury. Good sharp edges, proper binding adjustments, and a nice layer of wax make shifting weather conditions a lot easier.

### Mountain Features

The rugged terrain of the Wasatch Range is beautiful. However, it demands respect, and those who do not respect it are asking for trouble. Climbing a cliff or hiking to a peak to jump into a chute may seem exciting at the time, but unless you know the right route and understand the conditions, you may be putting your life in danger.

Steep peaks are conducive to avalanches and slides. Even with effective avalanche control, mountains still experience the occasional snowslide. You need to make certain you ski in bounds in areas that have active avalanche control. If you have the slightest doubt, check for proper signs. Resorts make an extra effort to ensure all areas are properly marked.

Glade skiing and boarding are wonderful experiences. Passing in and out of trees as you gently float in a field of snow is amazing. However, it is important that you take on these forests with skill and understanding of the terrain. Trees do not move and even a small strike can seriously injure you. If you have not done any glade skiing before, you might take a lesson or start on wide terrain and work your way into the glades.

Make certain that the resort has designated the area for glade skiing. If the trees you are skiing are not designated for exploration, there are going to be a lot of unseen obstacles. Even the most skilled rider will have difficulty navigating through a real forest. Consider the route you are taking and your level of experience before committing.

## Unmarked Terrain

A blanket of snow that all of us enjoy is covering some fairly nasty material. Jagged rocks, tree stumps, bushes, and other foliage are all hidden underneath. Unfortunately, those hidden elements can be exceptionally dangerous. These surprises can not only cause damage to your equipment but to your body as well.

## ☺ Tips and Tricks

Resorts try to mark the hazards on as much terrain as possible. In fact, they will put sticks, signs, and other markers whenever possible. Remember, early winter and late spring is when the most hazards exist. As the snow thins, more rough spots appear. Watch for the signs and watch where you are going.

Early in the season, obstacles are everywhere. While resorts make every effort to ensure the slopes are clear of any debris, they do not have control of gravity and the elements. The wind can blow an errant pinecone or a stray rock can fall onto the slopes. These small hazards can wreak havoc if you are not paying close attention. Later in the season, massive boulders and trees buried underneath snow can make dangerous surprises.

Snowboard or ski in control and keep your eyes fixed clearly on your path. Unmarked obstacles and mountain debris could be everywhere. Just like driving a car, you need to control your speed and anticipate changes on your path. You never know what is coming around the next turn.

## Out of Bounds

Around the slopes of your favorite resort, you will find orange ropes and poles designating the area boundary. These simple barriers can hardly keep a person out. A simple dip underneath the rope and you can be making tracks in uncut powder. However, this little diversion could mean your life.

Year after year around the world, people have died in avalanches or frozen to death while lost in terrain that is unmonitored and unsafe. The temptations of the open white country lure people, but you must resist. There is more than enough terrain for any visitor to Utah.

## ☺ Tips and Tricks

If you are serious about exploring the backcountry, the Utah Avalanche Center offers great educational programs to help you learn any aspect of avalanche safety. Besides the safety aspects of the program, they can teach you how to use a beacon and other important safety skills needed to survive a slide.

However, if that temptation is too large, you can certainly track down a professional guide who can show you the backcountry and ensure not only your safety but a great time. These guides will train you in avalanche safety, provide a good route, and give you all the Utah powder you can handle.

## Skier's Left and Right

Which way is left? Which way is right? It is all a matter of position and perspective. If you are trying to indicate where something is or where you are on the mountain, the method skiers and snowboarders use are the terms *skier's left* and *skier's right*.

Regardless of the direction, both are for indicating your left and right as you are facing downhill. In addition to providing direction, this is also a method for warning people who are in front of you on the slopes. If you are moving quickly on a trail and see a skier ahead of you, courtesy and safety warrants telling them you are coming.

Yell ahead, "on your left or on your right". This tells riders on which side you plan to pass. Remember, some people aren't too good at directions, so you want to give them ample warning and as much space as possible. However, a good warning will help them prepare for your approach and give you a safe passing lane.

## Maintain Control

For some, the thrill of speed is an exhilaration that only skiing or snowboarding can provide. As the adrenaline pumps and the wind swims across your face, it is an experience that few sports can provide. Sadly, it is this speed that can take the lives of not only

the skier or snowboarder but others who might be in their path.

Skiing and snowboarding are sports that require skill. As you progress from a novice, you gain the ability to control your board at different level of speeds. However, in this transitional period, it is easy to lose control and risk injury to yourself and others. Understand how to control your equipment and do not take terrain above your ability.

Many of the most serious injuries on a mountain are not caused by a person hitting an object—but rather, another person. Someone loses control of their speed or is going too fast for the terrain when some unsuspecting person enters their path. Ski in control and observe the signs posted by resorts.

The National Ski Patrol has a code established to help people understand the rules of the slopes. Much like those on the road, these codes have been established to help ensure everyone's safety on the slopes.

## The Responsibility Code

1. Always stay in control, and be able to stop or avoid other people or objects.
2. People ahead of you have the right-of-way. It is your responsibility to avoid them.
3. You must not stop where you obstruct a trail, or are not visible from above.
4. Whenever starting downhill or merging into a trail, look uphill and yield to others.
5. Always use devices to help prevent runaway equipment.
6. Observe all posted signs and warnings. Keep off closed trails and out of closed areas.

7. Prior to using any lift, you must have the knowledge and ability to load, ride, and unload safely.

Utah resorts use these valuable codes to set rules and guidelines for their slopes. Besides the common sense value of following the code, violators risk getting their ticket revoked and asked to leave the resort if they ski irresponsibly.

## Smart Style

Back in the early days of snowboarding, riders got their tickets pulled if they built a jump or were found riding off resort equipment. Things have certainly changed and now resorts build 40-foot jumps, place rails and tables on the slopes, and encourage people to fly into the air.

Out of this change, the National Ski Area Association has given snowboarders and terrain park enthusiasts their own separate code designed to improve safety and responsibility on the mountain. Smart Style was created for terrain parks to help prevent injury and to make their users more educated.

The following three messages are the key ideas behind Smart Style. Follow this mantra from the lift line throughout the park.

### Smart Style

1. *Look before you leap.*
   Scope around the jumps first, not over them. Know your landings are clear, and clear yourself out of the landing area quickly.

2. *Easy style it.*
   Start small and work your way up. (Inverted aerials not recommended.)

3. *Respect gets respect.*

Terrain parks are fun for both skiers and snowboarders. While these rules were set up initially for boarders, everyone enjoying the thrills and spills of the park should know Smart Style. It's less about the sport and more about common sense on the slopes.

## Ski or Snowboard Your Ability

People often ski or snowboard with friends and family and their differing abilities make no difference when the terrain is gentle. However, when the terrain gets steeper and the features become more challenging, inexperienced skiers and snowboarders are placed at risk. It is critical that everyone understands his or her own ability and what he or she can manage.

People caught up in the excitement of the moment may try to convince you to take a run that you are uncertain you can handle. By stating I know you can ski this, your friends seem to be demonstrating confidence in your ability. However, what they are really saying is that they are tired of skiing *easy* pistes.

For those who are new to the sport, never let anyone convince you to take a run which you feel exceeds your ability. You need to be comfortable and move at your own pace. What may seem easy to one person may be very challenging to another. You know your ability and you know what you can and can't do.

### ☺ Tips and Tricks

Your worst enemy on the mountain is fear. Simply stated, the difference between experts and beginners (besides ability) is fear. Experts have confidence in their capability, and as such, have no need to fear the slopes. Do not let fear prevent you from enjoying yourself. Just like any sport, with time your skills will improve and you can take on more difficult terrain.

Fear is how people get injured. They get on a run, become afraid, and seize up. This is the worst thing to do. If you find yourself on something too challenging, take a moment to stop and think about your options. Can you walk down? Can you carry your gear down? Can you climb up to another run? Can you traverse back and forth until you get to something easier?

Keep yourself calm and collected. You have no reason to fear anything. In the worst scenario, you can slide down on your rear end. Most times walking is the best option. You do not have to snowboard or ski down any run. Walking is something you have done since you were a toddler and is very manageable, even in boots, in the snow, on the steeper terrain.

It's easy for other people to tell you that you simply lack confidence or you are afraid. In fact, that may be part of the problem. However, you are still the one who has to control your equipment and poor confidence or fear can inhibit that control. Ski resorts do their best to make certain runs are clearly identified. Pay attention and stop before entering anything you have concerns about.

For a person who is more advanced, it may be frustrating to ride on terrain that is beneath your ability. Yet, placing your friends or family in a frightening and potentially dangerous situation is not a good idea. If you need to take on more challenging terrain, simply make a plan to meet together later. Designate some time for enjoying the slopes together and then slip out for some fun on an individual basis.

## ☺ Tips and Tricks

Cell phones work at many of the resorts. In addition, the FRS walkie-talkies are a terrific tool for keeping people connected. However, if you don't have either of these technologies, finding your friends or family can be difficult. Most of Utah's resorts are very large and you could spend a lot of time wandering around the resort.

If you get separated, make certain you have a communication plan with your friends or family. Select a spot to meet up at the end of the day. Choose a location that is easy to recognize and that everyone knows how to find. At the end of the day, everyone needs to be serious about being on time. A late person or no-show may end up having a rescue party sent out after them.

## Rating the Slopes

People who have never visited a mountain resort may still be familiar with the symbols used to mark difficulty. These icons of the slopes are easily recognizable and have been in place for years. These systems employed on the mountain help skiers and snowboarders quickly identify terrain based upon their skill level and experience.

Slopes are rated based upon their characteristics and are completely at the discretion of the resort. This means that one resort's black diamond might be another's blue square. Difficulty is all relative. However, most understand their customer very well and have taken this into consideration when designating the difficulty of a particular run.

The system is really designed as a warning for the beginner. Expert riders are not as concerned when a run is going to be more

▲ Aerials or easy turns, Utah resorts have you covered.

difficult. Yet, beginners need to understand how to create a safe and comfortable path down. They need to know if they are going to be going into something that is a bit over their head.

In this book, I have tried to help you find the right spots for your level of skiing. However, conditions and terrain can change and it may be helpful for beginners to chat with a mountain host or guide prior to hitting the slopes. This will ensure your safety and possibly get you a few recommendations on great groomed terrain.

Slopes are typically rated on steepness and terrain. More bumps and trees mean a higher difficulty rating. Things like grooming and traffic are also taken into consideration. Resorts measure the pitch and length as well. In the end, a run is designated a particular color because the resort knows the kind of skier who can handle it. Here is the North American Rating Guide.

## ● Easiest (Green Circle)

Runs with a green circle are typically quite gentle, flat, and featureless. They are often wide and exceptionally groomed to ensure no surprises. Many are usually positioned in locations that provide access to different parts of the mountain. Green runs also serve as places where people of all level of abilities can congregate.

Often you may see long green runs that traverse the mountain. These are called Cat Trails. Slope maintenance equipment uses these trails to access different parts of the mountain when they perform grooming. They can often be very flat and snowboarders will need to make certain they keep some speed to avoid a workout.

While green runs are the easiest, that does not mean people new to skiing or snowboarding should feel completely comfortable on them. Easiest runs still can have some vertical and can offer up small but manageable challenges to novice skiers. Until you have had some lessons and gained some competence in controlling your speed and stopping, you will want to stay on the beginner area of a mountain.

Green circles usually represent the smallest number of runs on the mountain. People who learn to ski or snowboard often progress to intermediate skills fairly quickly and these runs become unattractive. However, they often can be nice cruisers and a perfect spot to warm up your legs in the morning.

## ■ Intermediate (Blue Square)

Intermediate skiers and snowboarders are people who have had some time on their boards and feel comfortable exploring the mountain. Of all the difficulty levels, the blue run is the most varied and offers the most surprises. They can offer a little steeper terrain and even some small bumps.

In Utah, intermediate slopes are the most common variety at all the resorts. At some, as much as 50 percent of the mountain is dedicated to the blue. This means you will be able to find a lot of variety and options to explore as you build your skills.

Intermediate skiers and snowboarders are people confident in their ability to turn, control speed, and stop. They have had some time on their boards and are working on improving their skills. These runs cater to this learning by providing moderate challenges interspersed with areas of easier terrain. If you have newly progressed into the realm of intermediate skiing, you may want to take it slow.

## Advanced Intermediate (■ ■ Double Blue Square or ◆ Black on Blue)

The double blue is not used at every resort and sometimes can be represented as a blue square with a black diamond inside. Snowboarders and skiers looking to step up to black runs may find a double blue square a nice transition to help build confidence for the real black diamond runs.

The real question is what really differentiates the double blue from the black. This is purely a subjective call, but if you are not ready for a black, a double blue may also be too much of a challenge. It is simply a question of judgment and it is important for every

▲ Black diamond runs mean experience is necessary.

person to know his or her abilities before progressing to the next level.

### ◆ **Most Difficult** (Black Diamond)

Slopes marked with a black diamond are going to offer a lot of challenge for good riders and a lot of danger for novices. These runs are for veteran skiers and snowboarders who have the confidence to handle shifting terrain types and unexpected obstacles. A black diamond slope challenges riders to use their skills continuously.

Big bumps, narrow steeps, and ungroomed conditions are typical on the black diamond. Skiers and snowboarders with the confidence to take on black diamond runs

have been on their boards for a while and are prepared for anything. They may not always look good going down the mountain, but they can get down it without issue.

### ◆ ◆ **Experts Only** (Double Black Diamond)

Resorts try to capitalize on many different kinds of riders. They recognize that a majority of skiers and snowboarders spend most of their time on blue and green runs. However, each mountain tries to capture the mystique of the sport by providing areas that are some of the most difficult.

Trees, cliffs, chutes, bumps, and steeps make up the apex of mountain terrain. Skiers and snowboarders with the skill to handle the double black diamonds are in excellent physical shape and have outstanding ability and years of experience.

## Saving Some Bucks

There is no denying that skiing and snowboarding are expensive sports. The cost of equipment, lift tickets, lodging, and food all add up to a hefty price. At the end of the day, everyone likes to save a few dollars. The information below will not only help reduce the cost of your vacation, it could even end up paying for this book!

Utah is the best deal in skiing and snowboarding in the United States and possibly the world. Even the number one rated Deer Valley Resort is not as expensive as other luxury resorts. Lift ticket prices remain very affordable at all the resorts and there are innumerable methods to save money. Every resort in Utah has some method to save money.

The following tips will help you find some of these bargains. Remember, things change from year to year, and before any return visit to Utah, you may want to do a little detective work to see if a program you used in the past is still in operation. If this is your first visit, these clues will reveal some real savings.

### Discount Tickets

Most, if not all, the resorts offer discount programs annually to encourage locals to hit the slopes. From a ticket at a lower price to multiday discounts, each resort offers ways to save some money. The great thing about these programs is they are easy and will always save you something over what you will pay at the ticket window.

☺ **Tips and Tricks**

Season passes aren't just for locals. Resorts love to encourage season pass purchases, and at the end of the season, they start to sell them for the following year. Many discount these passes significantly for the following season, and early buyers can get them for what it might cost for a week of skiing during the regular season.

If you are planning a vacation to Utah and you know early enough, you may be able to purchase your pass for a steal. In addition, youth season tickets are very inexpensive. Many resorts discount them significantly to encourage families to ski together. Check the resort's web site to find out the prices, determine the number of days you plan on skiing, and then simply do the math.

Many of the resorts sell discounted tickets through the local grocery stores and sporting goods chains. Gas stations and convenience markets can also be a good source. Because it changes from year to year, a simple phone call to the customer service desk at one of these businesses can save you a bit of footwork. Here is a list of common places to check:

1. Local Ski and Snowboard Retailers (The best spot to check!)
2. National Sporting Goods Chains
3. Grocery Store Customer Service Counters
4. Convenience Stores (7-11, Maverick, etc.)
5. Hotel Concierge and Front Desks
   A couple things to note before you start. Park City resorts make a point not to sell discount tickets in Park City. Thus,

the surrounding area will be where you will find any discounts. Also note that some offers are for locals only. It might be good to ask about whether or not you are eligible. Last, some deals are in bundles so check to see how much you have to buy before committing.

## Kids and Novices

Most of the Utah resorts provide skiing and snowboarding for free or at significant discounts for the kids and people new to the sport. In fact, every year resorts make a special effort to encourage families to bring one and all. Providing not only financial incentives but many great services, they want to encourage everyone to learn to ride.

Starting around age six (and as old as 12), kids may be eligible for a free ticket. Every resort offers different programs.

For people new to skiing and snowboarding, some resorts offer free skiing and snowboarding on specific lifts, while others have

▼ Kids often ski for free.

certain times of the day where they open up terrain for new people to learn.

Each resort will feature their particular program on their web site and in their marketing material. As noted previously, some things do change and you may want to refer to your destination resort's web site to see their latest programs.

## First Day Free

Lumbering off an airliner doesn't usually inspire people to hit the slopes. Yet, the visage of the Wasatch Range may just inspire you to make a fast start. If you arrive early enough, you may be able to get some free warm-up runs in the afternoon. Many area resorts offer complimentary lift tickets when you show your boarding pass at the ticket office.

Of course with any *free* offer, there are rules and requirements. Each resort is different so be certain to check your destination to see if they offer the same day program. You may need to complete some paperwork prior to your arrival.

## Salt Lake Super Pass

The four Salt Lake City resorts have banded together to give you an amazing deal. If you are staying in Salt Lake, you can save a lot of money on your tickets. This 10-year-old program allows visitors to buy one day or multiday package.

Packages are often sold in conjunction with your hotel. However, you may be able to find it online as well as through various travel sites. You simply have to check with your lodging to see if they offer it. Regardless, the savings is great.

## Ski Utah

Utah's web site for skiing and snowboarding is www.skiutah.com. One of the great benefits of the site is its unending list of Hot Deals, which highlights resorts, lodging, and gear. They change the site throughout the season, and if you check it frequently, you may find a great deal for your destination!

## Rentals and Tunes

Often you can find a lot better deal on rental equipment, ski and snowboard tunes, and gear if you go away from the resorts. The local spots in the neighboring communities thrive because they offer better prices with the same quality and convenience. However, remember that you are going to sacrifice convenience for this savings.

## Using this Book

The ski and snowboard industry in Utah is constantly changing. Each resort strives to provide the best value for its customer. Advances in technology translate into new lifts, new mountain features, and other improvements. As such, it makes writing a book on the topic a touch challenging. The question arises about what will remain the same and what will change?

▼ Rental shops at the resorts provide convenience but are not as cheap.

DEER VALLEY RESORT

For this book to be valuable, the information contained within needs to remain enduring. Regardless of resort improvements, the data within must remain relevant and useful. Thus, I have had to avoid some significant topics and cut what might seem like useful information. I wanted my reader to get years of useful information from this book rather than a single season.

Things like trail maps and prices shift slightly from year to year. Restaurants come and go. The Internet provides amazing resources for vacation planning. You only need to click a couple of buttons to find great information about any of these resorts. However, even with all this information, do you really know the mountain?

Though the snowfall may change from year to year, the mountain surface and layout remains a steady constant. The landscape changes very little, and while resorts sometimes expand from year to year, they rarely remove anything. The details here are based on those things that rarely change.

This book is a tool to help you not only get comfortable with your destination but get the most from your vacation. With the valuable tips and tricks, the details about the mountain, and a good guide to what each resort offers, you can use the information here to plan your day of skiing or snowboarding.

Whether you are taking your first lessons or you plan on jumping off a few cliffs during your vacation, the information contained within will help you get there faster and easier. I have also included a number of tips and tricks to help you avoid some of the minor pitfalls of your visit. It is my hope that after spending the time to read about a resort, you will take the time to explore all it has to offer.

## The Internet

There is no greater resource in our time for information. With this understanding, Utah's resorts provide very good data about their accommodations, facilities, and other aspects you might want to know about prior to your visit.

This book is designed to give you more than what you can find on the web. Details about where to go and how to get the most from your visit are what I wanted to deliver. Here are the primary resort links to help with your vacation planning:

**Ski Utah** at www.skiutah.com
**Alta** at www.alta.com
**Beaver Mountain** at www.skithebeav.com
**Brian Head** at www.brianhead.com
**Brighton** at www.skibrighton.com
**Deer Valley** at www.deervalley.com
**Park City** at www.parkcitymountain.com
**Powder Mountain** at www.powder
   mountain.net
**Solitude** at www.skisolitude.com
**Snowbasin** at www.snowbasin.com
**Snowbird** at www.snowbird.com
**Sundance** at www.sundanceresort.com
**The Canyons** at www.thecanyons.com
**Wolf Mountain** at www.wolfmountain
   eden.com

## Trail Maps

While reviewing the content for each resort, you may want to keep a trail map nearby. Whether you access one from the Internet or grab one upon arrival, the trail map is a key component to helping you find your way around the mountain. Unfortunately, resorts change their lifts and sometimes the names of runs, so I have done my best to give you good

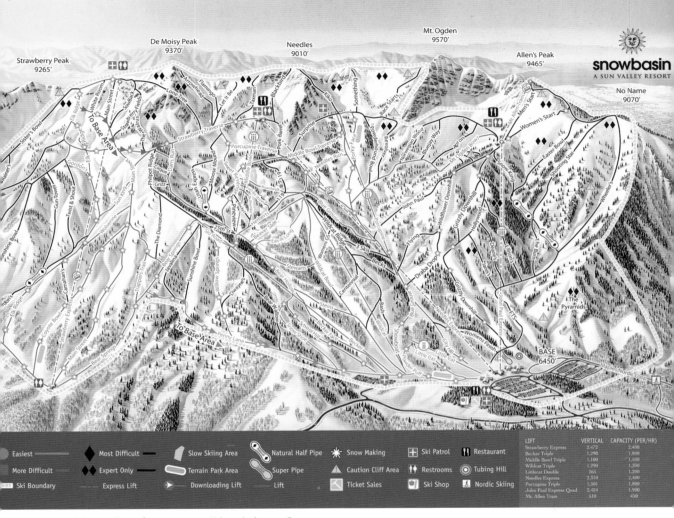

| LIFT | VERTICAL | CAPACITY (PER/HR) |
|---|---|---|
| Strawberry Express | 2,472 | 2,400 |
| Becker Triple | 1,290 | 1,800 |
| Middle Bowl Triple | 1,100 | 1,500 |
| Wildcat Triple | 1,290 | 1,200 |
| Littlecat Double | 265 | 1,200 |
| Needles Express | 2,510 | 2,400 |
| Porcupine Triple | 1,501 | 1,800 |
| John Paul Express Quad | 2,424 | 1,900 |
| Mt. Allen Tram | 510 | 450 |

Legend:
- ◆ Most Difficult — Slow Skiing Area — ⬡ Natural Half Pipe — ✳ Snow Making — ✚ Ski Patrol — Ⅱ Restaurant
- ▬ Easiest
- ◆◆ Expert Only — Terrain Park Area — Super Pipe — ▲ Caution Cliff Area — Restrooms — Tubing Hill
- More Difficult
- ▦ Ski Boundary — Express Lift — ➤ Downloading Lift — Lift — Ticket Sales — Ski Shop — Nordic Skiing
- Express Lift

▲ Resorts change from year to year. Pick up the latest trail map on your visit. (Courtesy of Snowbasin)

directions to the suggested areas of the mountain to explore.

Runs are identified by name and on occasion I have cited the lift that is nearby. Lifts are far more likely to change than run names because resorts are always working to improve their infrastructure. Yet, it is entirely possible for one, the other, or both to change between seasons.

# 1

# Alta Mountain Resort

## About the Resort

There are magical locations around our globe where people make a pilgrimage to find enlightenment. Whether it is for spiritual renewal or a quest for personal salvation, these special places provide contentment, peace, and unrestrained joy for the seeker. One of these destinations is Alta (which is pronounced AL-ta, like the name Al, not AHL-ta).

Nestled at the top of Little Cottonwood Canyon, the base of the mountain seems to embrace visitors. Alta's towering peaks appear to be the fingers of a giant holding magic in the palm of his hand. This magic is the lightest, deepest, and most delightful powder Utah has to offer.

Annually, people from around the globe return again and again to ski Alta. Not unlike a pilgrimage, these visitors come several times a season and consider it their spiritual home. This tradition has continued for nearly 70 years and it only takes a single visit to understand this calling.

While Park City ties its history to mining, Alta is a rustic resort with a long history tied to skiing. Some of the first turns on skis in Utah were done here. Alta started as a mountain mining town, but avalanches and fire took their toll in the late 19th century. By 1937 skiing had become the principal industry of the town.

Since that time, Alta has been in continuous operation as a ski resort. As the Salt Lake Valley grew so did the resort, which became a major destination for locals wanting to experience this exciting new sport. While innovations in lifts and facilities have changed the

P.O. Box 8007
Alta, UT 84092
**Web:** www.alta.com
**E-mail:** info@alta.com
**Main:** 801-359-1078
**Snow Report:**
  801-572-3939
**Ski School:**
  801-359-1078
**RESORT STATISTICS**
**Peak Elevation:** 10,550 feet
  (3,215 meters)
**Base Elevation:** 8,530 feet
  (2,600 meters)
**Vertical Drop:** 2,020 feet
  (615 meters)
**Area:** 2,200 acres
  (890 hectares)
**Night Skiing:** No

▲ Alta is famous for the back-country-style terrain within its boundaries.

resort, the powder and mountain—for which it is famous—remain the same.

## About the Mountain

There are few areas in the state of Utah equal to the picture perfect setting that is Alta. Towering peaks, jagged cliffs, and abundant pines are what come to mind when imagining a ski resort. However, the true magic of Alta is not in its landscape but its amazing powder.

As one of the highest resorts along the Wasatch Front, Alta sees some of the largest snowfall annually and gets the best of the powder of any resort. Its natural bowl-like formation seems to harness as much of the snow as possible from each storm and leaves skiers in abundant, deep, dry Utah snow.

There is little question that Alta is truly one of the best places to find powder in Utah, and if that is your goal, you would be crazy not to grab your skis and experience it after a plentiful storm. Even with crowds, there is ample to go around.

The mountain is divided into two separate base areas. The Albion Base caters to all kinds of skiers from beginners to cliff jumpers. It has the most diverse terrain on the mountain and is a good starting place if you are new to the sport. The Wildcat Base is only for intermediate to expert skiers.

One of the most controversial things about Alta is its refusal to allow snowboarding. People see the epic mountains and legendary powder and cry foul. However, there is a real rationale behind this decision, and before getting upset, boarders need to appreciate that there is no bias against their sport or their culture.

Alta was formed by glaciers and from this geology came a terrain that is very steep and filled with flat spots. Any skier who has spent time in some of Alta's steeps can testify to the amount of hiking, pushing, and poling required. Many of the best spots involve walking.

Unfortunately, snowboarding does not lend itself well to hiking and long flats. Boarders are forced to drag along when the terrain gets flat, while skiers can skate or push with poles. For Alta to support snowboarding safely and effectively, millions of dollars in lifts and landscaping would be necessary.

▼ The views at Alta are simply breathtaking.

RANAE BUNKER

▲ Hiking is not uncommon to get to Alta's most challenging terrain.

▲ Terrain to explore as far as the eye can see.

With this in mind, the resort decided to take a philosophical approach to the business. While they were one of the first resorts to allow snowboarding, their motto has always been "Alta is for skiers." The long history of the resort is closely tied to skiing, and Alta determined that it should keep to the motto and keep out snowboarding.

Naturally, they do not want to discourage the sport of snowboarding and have partnered with Snowbird through the Alta-Snowbird Connection so visitors to Alta can easily get to a mountain for boarding. Nonetheless, Alta remains exclusively for skiers. It is part of their heritage and they plan to keep it that way.

## ● Easiest Terrain

While experts may flock to Alta, the resort welcomes beginner skiers and provides great terrain to start skiing. From the Sunnyside Triple, you can find a diverse and interesting collection of green runs. In addition, the Cecret Double also provides options for beginning skiers.

Beginners might want to start on Crooked Mile and work their way from the top of the Sunnyside lift over the different terrain. You can explore slightly different yet moderate runs as your confidence and skills improve. One thing to note is that the trail map shows the Albion Double as an option, but currently this is only open when traffic at the mountain warrants it.

## ☺ Tips and Tricks

If you are new to skiing and want to experiment on the slopes, Alta offers a program called Ski Free After 3. This program lets anyone pick up a lift ticket and ride the Sunnyside Triple from 3–4 PM. In addition, Alta's rope tows are free all day long.

## ■ Intermediate Terrain

Alta provides the intermediate skier with a lot of great choices. The Collins Quad delivers a lot of vertical for those on the higher end of the intermediate spectrum. Runs from the Wildcat Base have a bit more steep than a typical blue and intersect with a lot of black runs.

▼ Get yourself ready at the top for Alta's amazing snow.

▲ The powder at Alta is world famous.

Those just becoming a blue skier may want to consider the Sugarloaf Quad with its gentler yet beautifully groomed runs. The Albion Base provides skiing of all types, but the runs off Sugarloaf are much easier than those on the Supreme Triple. You may want to get a few warm-up runs before hitting Supreme.

Intermediate skiers wanting a taste of Alta's famous powder can follow the Ballroom Traverse and then drop into Ballroom for some wonderful snow. Before you take the plunge, look up and see if you can spot some of the extreme skiers dropping into the Baldy Chutes.

### ◆ Advanced Terrain

From the Wildcat Base, advanced skiers will uncover abundant options from challenging blues to aggressive expert terrain. Depending on your skill level, you can really discover anything you like. Take the Collins Quad all the way to the top and then explore some of the best skiing in Utah.

More aggressive skiers will want to prove their muster on the Alta's legendary High Rustler. The run is super steep and usually bumped up and takes a lot of a traverse skiing to access. However, it is the stuff legends are made of and you will want to make certain you take a least one run if you want to come back with bragging rights.

Off the Wildcat Double you will find some of Alta's most accessible expert terrain. Even better, this part of the mountain does not receive a lot of traffic and you will find empty lift lines with a number of wonderful challenges. It is especially good on a powder day as everyone else heads up to the top of the mountain.

### ☺ Tips and Tricks

If you find a long line on the Collins Quad, hop on to the Wildcat Double to get a warm-up run or two and you will quickly discover

the line at the base has diminished. In addition, you can even pick up the Collins Quad at mid-mountain. However, you may have to wait a while for an empty chair.

## ◆ ◆ Experts Only Terrain

Alta does not define any of its terrain as double black because, for the most part, the issue is moot. If you take a look at it and still want to ski it, you obviously know what you are doing. The mountain does not hide its vertical rocky terrain and it takes expert skills just to access much of it.

This mountain is legendary for its aggressive steeps and backcountry skiing. Be prepared to pull off the old skis and do some hiking if you want to really get the true Alta experience. Cliffs, bowls, chutes, and trees are going to be found in the upper elevations, and long traverses to a hike are not unusual.

In addition, secret spots are everywhere at Alta. People make a point of marking up trail maps and figuring out routes to get to the perfect untracked powder. Trading stories about the deep and steep or a snorkel day are common among Alta aficionados.

## ☺ Tips and Tricks

It is well known that Alta has an open boundary policy. What this means is you can ski out of bounds but you take the risk. If you get caught in an avalanche or get lost, you will pay for the rescue and any other costs (possibly your life).

As tempting as that uncut snow is, *do not* cross boundaries unless you are a seasoned expert with backcountry experience and avalanche training or have a guide in tow. Alaska Mountain Guides at the base can arrange tours of the backcountry if you want to do this kind of skiing.

## Cruisers

You can find some great cruisers across the mountain, but the best are off the Supreme Triple. Runs like Big Dipper and Rock N' Roll are wide, have a nice pitch, and provide great speed with no bumps. If you want to extend your run, keep going to the bottom to the Sunnyside area where you will find great green cruisers.

Off the Sugarloaf Quad you can find a great number of cruising options. This part of the mountain is quite open and nicely groomed. From Little Dipper over to the Devil's Elbow, there are some smooth cruises to be found. Again, you can lengthen your run and get more turns if you choose to ride to the base.

Over on the Collins Quad, Mambo to Main Street is great fun and offers a nice cruise with a prospect of speed. Whether taking turns or simply looking for an open run, this suggests a nice ride. At the bottom, you may want to stick with Meadow if you don't want to continue cruising without bumps or steeps.

## Bumps

Alta does have bumps but you have to know where to find them. If you want to get warmed up, hit Vicky's off the Supreme Triple. The run is relatively short but the bumps get nicely formed. In addition, you are close to some of the bigger moguls on Challenger or Number 9 Express once you get your legs pumped.

Once the fresh snow has been skied off, you can find some seriously pitched steeps with bumps off the High Traverse. Just ski along until you see something that appeals to you and drop off either side. The ridgeline is filled with challenges of all types. The big bumps here are among the toughest.

## Trees and Steeps

For the intermediate skier looking to get some experience in the woods, seek out the Yellow Bear Trail. It is not marked on the map, but if you traverse from the Sugarloaf Quad over on Supreme Access, you will find various cabins and a small hill. Drop into that forest and pop out just above the Sugarloaf loading area. Be careful to watch out for the river and some holes.

If you want to find more aggressive tree skiing, a hike over to Catherine's is in order. Take the Supreme Triple and climb up to the top of the Catherine's area. The farther in you ski, the more vertical you lose. However, the trees are great over to the edge of the East Castle area.

Steeps are all over Alta, and as mentioned, High Rustler is one of the most notorious runs for this kind of challenge. In fact, they put a ski catcher at the bottom of the run for those who lose control on this challenging run. Eddie's High Nowhere and anything else on the High Traverse is going to give you vertical you won't soon forget.

## Powder

Where isn't the powder at Alta? On a big snow day, the perfect powder hole can be found literally anywhere. However, the mountain gets cut up very fast. Those who know powder skiing want to be at Alta after a dump. If you are insistent on making first tracks, you will need to get to the mountain early.

Westward Ho off the Wildcat Double is possibly your best shot for uncut snow as most people are heading up to the summit of the mountain. Still, if you ski too far over, you may have to hike back to the base. On busy days you may get lucky and find a truck doing the rounds to bring back wayward powder hogs.

After experiencing Alta in a dump, you will suddenly decide you know where the best powder shots are and what holes you want to keep to yourself. You see, Alta is a big mountain and everyone has his or her own stories to share. It is part of what makes this resort special. Even newcomers discover their own Alta.

## Other Activities

One of the distinct advantages of skiing Alta is the Alta-Snowbird Connection. In addition to all the wonderful terrain you can ski at Alta, you can purchase a pass that will allow you to ski Snowbird as well. This will more than double the amount of skiable terrain and has many other great benefits.

The two resorts are amazingly well connected. You can literally stand at the top of the Sugarloaf Quad and ski over to Snowbird. Thus, you can switch back and forth throughout the day without any trouble. You get the best of both worlds, all the great skiing at Alta and access to some of the best powder skiing at The Bird.

Families with snowboarders and skiers can get the pass and meet their snowboarding counterparts for lunch at one of Snowbird's excellent restaurants. Then you can choose to continue skiing at Snowbird or return to Alta. Either way, there is a convenient bus that runs between both resorts.

Alta also offers great Nordic skiing. They have a 5km groomed track that weaves in and out between the Albion and Wildcat Bases. It's the perfect diversion from alpine skiing as it is at the mountain but outside where most people ski. Thus, you can get a peaceful break with the beauty of Alta on a track centered in the heart of the resort.

## Lodging

While the Lodges at Alta are independently owned, they are very much a part of the resort. And while their exteriors may look aged and a touch worn, they provide excellent accommodations for visitors. In fact, if you plan a trip to Alta, you need to book well in advance because the resort attracts returning guests.

Many of the people who frequent Alta are people who have committed a lifetime to this resort. The lodging is repeatedly filled with people who trek to the resort year after year after year. The five base lodges are focused on providing all-inclusive packages including breakfast and dinner. They fill quickly so plan ahead.

If you find Alta is booked solid, you can certainly check with Snowbird and their world-class accommodations. If you do not need to stay at the mountain, a short drive into the Salt Lake Valley will find unlimited lodging options. Either way, a visit to Alta does not require a stay at Alta.

## Restaurants

For the most part, on-mountain restaurants at Alta offer your standard ski variety in cafeteria form. Burgers, chili, soup, and other fried goodies can be piled up on a tray and shared with your crew. People really don't come to Alta to eat. However, hidden on the third floor of the Watson Shelter, there is a pleasant surprise waiting for you.

The Collins Grill is a full-service restaurant with booties for your feet, baskets for your clothes, and delectable delights for your stomach. With spectacular views and stunning food, this new restaurant is really a welcome break from standard cafeteria food offered at the resort. However, it is pricey.

If you prefer your sustenance in liquid form, visit Alta Java at the Albion Base. It is a great little coffee shop with a lot of character and comfortable chairs for relaxing. Skiers can get a quick warm-up, take a bathroom break, and get a good jolt of caffeine to keep going.

▲ Take a coffee break or grab a snack at Alta Java.

# 2

# Beaver Mountain

## About the Resort

Scientists remain skeptical about the possibility of time travel. However, one visit to Logan's Beaver Mountain and they may change their mind. Like stepping back 30 years in the ski industry, Beaver Mountain has retained all the charm and comfort of the old mom-and-pop resorts of yesteryear.

Time stands still at Beaver. You can find people still skiing in blue jeans, sporting mullets, and wearing down vests. You will discover short lift lines, homemade brownies, and families having barbecues out of the back of their trucks. Best of all, Beaver has not let time influence their prices.

Part of its charm is the simple and comfortable surroundings. There is nothing fancy or pretentious about Beaver Mountain. This doesn't mean the surroundings are old or run down. Quite the contrary, everything is well maintained. The resort is clean and efficient and their grooming is immaculate.

Deep up Logan Canyon, Beaver Mountain has been in constant operation and family-owned from the 1930s. Since that time, Beaver has retained a lot of its original character while still being an updated and contemporary resort. You will see that it delivers few crowds, friendly people, and affordable skiing.

Beaver retains a lot of its classic character from the locals who frequent the resort. On more than one occasion, I could hear people yelling greetings to one another. The lift operators had smiles on their faces and welcomed me every time they handed me a seat.

40000 East Highway 89
Garden City, UT 84028
**Web:** www.skithebeav.com
**E-mail:** info@skithebeav.com
**Main:** 435-753-0921
**Snow Report:**
  435-753-4822
**Ski and Snowboard
  School:** 435-753-0921
**RESORT STATISTICS**
**Peak Elevation:**
  8,860 feet (2,700 meters)
**Base Elevation:**
  7,200 feet (2,195 meters)
**Vertical Drop:** 1,660 feet
  (505 meters)
**Area:** 664 acres
  (269 hectares)
**Night Skiing and
  Snowboarding:** No

▲ Beaver has the same great Utah terrain as the Salt Lake resorts.

In fact, I found myself feeling like part of the resort by the end of the day.

With Beaver Mountain you can enjoy all the character and quality of simpler times. Leaving behind the trappings of all the larger resorts, Beaver strives to provide a great environment for locals and destination skiers to enjoy by returning to a simpler time. Perhaps traveling backward in time isn't necessary after all.

## About the Mountain

One of the most surprising things about Beaver is how much skiing and snowboarding is available. At first glance, you might assume this is a tiny resort. Yet, many turns later you will find that the two mountains and the wide runs accommodate a lot of skiers and snowboarders.

The design of the trail system spreads people around the resort creating very few pockets of congestion or crowds. There is a little bit of everything for everyone all over the mountain. Beginner, intermediate, and expert skiers do have spots specifically dedicated to them. However, you can find a bit of every color all over the mountain.

The lifts servicing the resort are simple and easy to access. Two triples and two doubles provide excellent coverage to the entire terrain. It is a lengthy trek if you want to go from one side to the other. Nonetheless, this only provides an opportunity to get in a few longer runs.

▲ Locals give Beaver a warm and friendly atmosphere.

## ☺ Tips and Tricks

Lift tickets are purchased in a small building at the bottom of the resort. If you take the Little Beaver Double and follow the Goat Trail to Harry's Dream Triple, you don't have to climb the hill to get to the lift. Even better, your first run is a nice short warm-up.

One thing that will surprise visitors is the terrific grooming. Beaver strives to provide perfection on their slopes. Fresh cut corduroy surfaces are easy to find. Even in early season, rocks and brown spots are rare. They spend a lot of time making certain that the best possible ski surface is provided for their customer.

While the mountain may not be massive, it certainly provides more than enough terrain for the entire family to enjoy. The terrain is diverse and accommodates skiers of most levels. The mountain is well maintained and everyone will certainly have a lot of fun!

## ● Easiest Terrain

Beaver Mountain really does a lot to accommodate beginners. Their perfectly groomed runs and large number of greens provide new skiers and snowboarders time to learn and get comfortable. The small crowds and friendly nature of the resort will really help novices adapt and excel.

▲ Beaver is charming and uncomplicated.

Beginners can start on a rope tow or the Little Beaver Double. All of the terrain in this area is great for learning. It is long enough to give you the confidence you need to get comfortable but short enough to keep you from getting exhausted. As your skill improves, you can begin to explore other parts of the mountain.

Beaver has many long pistes that traverse its two mountains. This is a fun way to see a lot more of the resort while still staying on the easiest terrain. These nice long runs help you feel like you really are getting the most from your day.

Green riders and skiers will want to avoid the Beaver Face Double completely. Marge's Triple does have some pleasant runs for connecting, but everything below is for more advanced skiers. If you are up for a bigger test, take a ride to the top of Harry's Dream Triple and take Gentle Ben for a long, tranquil ride down.

▲ Tree skiing is great at Beaver.

## ■ Intermediate Terrain

Marge's Triple and Harry's Dream Triple both provide a lot of options for the intermediate skier or snowboarder. However, where you sit in the intermediate spectrum will determine which area of the mountain that you want to explore.

For those who consider themselves just new intermediate skiers, you may want to avoid Harry's Dream Triple. The blue runs do have a bit more steep than you may find on a typical blue run, and unless you know how to control your speed effectively, this could be a concern.

The runs on Marge's Triple are very comfortable for all intermediates. Take a nice glide down Shady or gentle ride through Ted's Rock, and you will find your skills are not only improving, you are really enjoying the resort.

### ◆ Advanced Terrain

Surprisingly, Beaver is not without some expert terrain. In fact, it has a number of great choices and some runs that might defy even the most seasoned veterans. The Beaver Face Double is effectively designed to serve only black skiing and it only takes a single ride up to see this is the case.

The North Face and South Face provide challenging moguls and some decent steep terrain for experts to test their muster. The entire face area may not be lengthy. However, what it loses in vertical, it gains in steeps.

### ◆ ◆ Experts Only Terrain

Sometimes it is good to take a day off. Jumping from cliffs, burying yourself in powder, or slamming knees into the bumps can really get exhausting. Perhaps, you need some rest and could take time to enjoy a nice cruiser. Maybe you want some pleasant tree skiing. Beaver is a great way to lighten up and find a more relaxed pace.

Besides, Beaver Mountain doesn't really have the kind of terrain suited to the experts looking for extreme skiing and snowboarding. Their mountain is small enough to offer some challenges, but in the end, this is not a destination for double black skiers. On the other hand, that doesn't mean you won't have fun.

## Cruisers

Marge's Triple is home to the best cruisers on the mountain, and anyone looking for some nicely groomed terrain can pick any number of runs to have a wonderful time. Shady, Red Tail, Ted's Rock, and Sunshine are excellent and maintained to ensure a smooth surface.

From the top of Harry's Dream Triple, explore Gentle Ben for a long and smooth ride all the way to the bottom. It intersects with Dead Horse on the map but it is still part of the entire run. It is gentler but still nice when you just want to make some turns.

### ☺ Tips and Tricks

If you are an advanced rider and you are taking Gentle Ben home on your new board, you may want to avoid Grand Canyon. The run has some steep side walls and bits of debris do fall and decorate the ground even in heavy snow. Just hang over to the left and go around it and follow the Easiest Way Down signs.

▲ Like Fine Wine,
Beaver improves with age.

## Bumps

Beaver provides bump lovers with many choices. There are many great options on either side of the resort. Off the Beaver Face Double, the South Face seems to get the best carved moguls. On Harry's Dream Triple, Ego Trip at the top is a popular bump spot. In fact, they get pretty impressive in size.

From the top, you can find the upper part of Lue's. It gets a lot of traffic and develops some nicely carved moguls. There is not a lot on the other mountain, so you may want to hang around Harry's or Beaver Face if your focus is banging the moguls.

## Trees and Steeps

One of the most distinctive features of Beaver is its abundant tree skiing. The folks at the mountain spend a lot of time in the off-season creating glades and optimal conditions for skiing and boarding in the trees. The end result is a place that is not only magical but also extensive.

Both sides of Marge's Triple have pines, cedars, and aspens spread evenly for the perfect tree run. On the other hand, Citizen Kent's has been specifically cut for tree skiing. Beaver spends the off-season glading the area to give you the best experience and the best turns possible.

There is nothing incredibly steep but the Beaver Face has its challenges. There are some great runs to explore that do have adequate vertical for the steeper skier. Try Lue's or North Face for the best steeps available on the mountain.

## Powder

The Logan area does get a bit colder than the other resorts. However, this means they will also get some of the drier and lighter powder. The whole resort gets excellent snow throughout the winter, and while they may not have the massive vertical of some other places, they also don't have the traffic.

Even days after a storm, people can still find fresh track powder. Whether it is skiing through the beautiful trees or finding a few nice steeps, Beaver Mountain gets the same wonderful Utah snow and has a lot of places to show it off.

▼ You won't find crowds at Beaver Mountain.

▲ Riders head to the Rodeo Grounds to test their skills.

Advanced skiers and snowboarders will find the steep and deep off the Beaver Face. Lue's, Stans, and Harry's Hollow are also good choices if you're looking for fresh snow. Fine Wine is an excellent little jaunt in between the two mountains and it doesn't see as much traffic. You may be able to make some fresh tracks there.

## Snowboarding

Beaver encourages and invites snowboarders into their fold. In fact, they have a fairly extensive terrain park and their nicely groomed runs are suited perfectly for wide turns and fast riding. However, their terrain is not really suited to beginning riders. When there is enough snow, there are two parks. One is smaller and one is called the Rodeo Grounds.

The Rodeo Grounds has all the same features the bigger areas have but with less traffic. The park is nicely placed near the edge of the resort to keep errant skiers and snowboarders from wandering in accidentally. Off Marge's Triple, this spot does accommodate all levels of riders but is really for someone with more experience.

## Other Activities

While there is nothing specifically at the resort, Logan Canyon plays host to many different winter activities. The Forest Service provides numerous Nordic trails near Beaver Mountain. In addition, you can explore the beauty of the area by snowmobile. Rentals can be found at Beaver Creek Lodge, which is very close and also located in Logan Canyon. For information go to www.beavercreeklodge.com.

## Lodging

There is no lodging at Beaver Mountain but you do not need to go far to find great accommodations. To the south, Logan is a college town with many options for visitors and is only about 40 minutes

▼ Tailgating is not just a football activity in Utah.

away from the resort. Logan has a lot of great restaurants and even a few bars for a small Utah town.

To the north, visitors will find the cerulean Bear Lake. This beautiful resort area is a very popular destination in both the summer and winter. During the winter, people escape from the urban life to snowmobile, Nordic ski, and of course, ski at Beaver. The resort's close proximity to the Bear Lake makes it a perfect place to stay.

## Restaurants

Because you are stepping back in time, you are also going back to the foods of yesteryear. The small A-frame shack lodge provides comfortable lunch tables and good typical ski fare. Fresh burgers and sandwiches along with homemade brownies can easily fill up the hole in your stomach.

During my visit, more than one person was brown bagging. In addition, I saw loads of people tailgating and making the day at the slopes a family event. Food is not the big focus at Beaver; rather, the emphasis is the time you get to spend with people on and off the mountain.

# Brian Head Resort

**3**

## About the Resort

There are contrasts in nature that epitomize the beautiful aspects of skiing and snowboarding. The rich dark greens of pines against the blue sky are but one example of how nature paints a spectacular picture. Brian Head takes these same elements and adds a drop of red into the mixture for spectacular results.

Situated in southern Utah among the red rock cliffs and formations, Brian Head almost seems like an anomaly. Cedar Breaks National Monument is only a short drive from the Brian Head parking lot, and the view from the top shows deep reds contrasting against green and white. This resort stands unique among resorts not only in Utah but the world.

The highest of any base in the state, Brian Head also gets its fair share of snow. Nearly 400 inches fall here every year, and as such, it is a popular destination for skiers and snowboarders in an area that is normally known for its desert. Residents of Southern California and Nevada trek a short three hours from Las Vegas to find real winter fun.

There is no shortage of enjoyment at Brian Head. The resort not only is a great place to ski and snowboard, but you can try sleigh rides, snowmobiling, cross-country skiing, and tubing. A visit to this resort is about exploring plenty of winter activities and enjoying time with your family.

Family friendly is really the key to this resort. For more than 40 years, the people at Brian Head have been hosting families who make

329 South Highway 143
P.O. Box 190008
Brian Head, UT 84719

**Web:** www.brianhead.com

**E-mail:** request@ brianhead.com

**Main:** 435-677-2035

**Snow Report:** 435-677-2035

**Ski and Snowboard School:** 435-677-2035

**RESORT STATISTICS**

**Peak Elevation:** 11,307 feet (3,446 meters)

**Base Elevation:** 9,600 feet (2,926 meters)

**Vertical Drop:** 1,707 feet (520 meters)

**Area:** 500 acres (202 hectares)

**Night Skiing and Snowboarding:** Yes

▲ Brian Head is a great place to learn.

an annual trek up from the south to enjoy it all. Its wide selection of activities and nice accommodations make it a popular choice. Its convenient location and size make it an easy selection for a winter vacation.

Brian Head is not only convenient but also affordable. Lift lines are rare and access to the resort is convenient. They also offer many different packages for visitors. From complete equipment rentals, lessons, and tickets to kids' camps, their goal is to ensure everyone goes home with a smile on their face.

## ☺ Tips and Tricks

Brian Head recognizes that their resort is primarily a destination for families. Thus, they have created kids' camps, which will take youngsters from 6 weeks to 12 years old. This is a great way to ensure both the kids and the parents have fun!

The camp is integrated with the ski school, and children are taught at their own pace and provided lunch. It combines a fully licensed day care facility with the fun of a ski school. This means the kids have fun, learn to ski, and are tired at the end of the day.

There are not many resorts where you can visit an amazing national monument and then spend an afternoon on the slopes. Bringing together beautiful scenery, a family-friendly atmosphere, and numerous choices for activities, Brian Head is a great destination where everyone can find something to enjoy.

## About the Mountain

Numerous resorts in Utah provide places for beginning skiers to get started. However, how many can claim they have an entire mountain devoted to beginners? Brian Head lays claim to this fame by providing a complete area for novice skiing and snowboarding.

There are two bases at Brian Head. Navajo Peak is the learning zone of the resort and focuses completely on helping get new riders on their boards. The other base has the Brian Head Peak and the Giant Steps area to offer the more challenging terrain.

▼ While located in Southern Utah, Brian Head gets a lot of fresh powder.

▲ Brian Head has the highest base of all the Utah resorts.

On either side, riders will find that the mountain is wide open and great for making turns. Snowboarders will be especially pleased with its great terrain for wide turns, natural walls, and great drops. Skiers will find a lot of the mountain really suitable for speed with some fun cruisers.

The resort has not made an investment into new high-speed lift technology like many of the other resorts in Utah, but it does not seem to be a problem. Even on a busy day, crowds are not an issue. The busiest weekends of the season have relatively short lift lines, and because they have two mountains for skiers, people are spread out.

Brian Head is not very large but it does provide a nice layout of different terrain. You can find a little bit of everything. Bumps, steeps, cruisers, and other elements of a high-quality resort are represented effectively. You can even find some fun surprises if you look hard enough.

Brian Head features very inexpensive season passes. If you are planning a visit for a week or more, you may want to check the early season rates on a season pass. It could save you a lot of money and provide you with that reason to make more than one trip a year.

In all, Brian Head is not Utah's biggest or most exciting offering but it is a great all-around resort for a family vacation. Everyone will have fun skiing and snowboarding its great terrain and then have a wonderful time off the slopes!

## ● Easiest Terrain

As previously noted, Brian Head is the only resort in the state that commits almost an entire mountain to green skiing. The Navajo Peak area is all green except for two runs. Thus, you can easily find a place to get a relaxed starting point and build up your confidence.

The Pioneer Double is the training lift and services three starting runs. Once you have progressed enough to stop and turn effectively, take the Navajo Chair to explore many of the gentle runs positioned directly off the chair but not under it. Snowboarders can find a beginning terrain park off to skier's right.

If you happen to be over at the Giant Steps Lodge, there is one run on either side of the Blackfoot Triple. Desbah is to skier's left and Heavenly Daze is to skier's right. Both are nice runs and perfect for beginners who might be skiing or snowboarding with the remainder of the family.

## ■ Intermediate Terrain

The Giant Steps Triple has long wide-open runs that seem to be popular with snowboarders. If you are a new blue skier, head over to The Dunes Triple and you will find smaller crowds, great selections, and easier runs.

### ☺ Tips and Tricks

While there is quite a bit of intermediate terrain at Brian Head, you will want to keep a sharp eye on the landscape and the trail signs. The resort has a tendency to intermingle a lot of their black runs and blue runs together.

This can be nice as you can ski or snowboard with riders of varied levels. However, it can spell disaster if somebody goes somewhere they don't belong. Be certain to examine the trail map closely before heading to the slopes.

If you are an edgier intermediate and looking to push yourself to the advanced level, hang out on the Roulette Triple. There is less traffic and the options open up with a few blue and easier blacks to test your skill level.

### ◆ Advanced Terrain

While the expert terrain at Brian Head is not as challenging as some resorts, there are certainly some runs that will test the advanced skiers. The Dunes Triple has several short but bumpy runs that make for a nice workout and then a quick ride back to the top.

The Giant Steps Triple is really a great mix for the more advanced snowboarding crowd. It has a lot of wide-open and steep runs for great turns on a nice pitch. In addition, two of the resort's three snowboard parks are located off this lift.

The Roulette Triple does provide some black runs as well. Wild Ride and First Tracks are fun and playful runs worth exploring. However, if you are a real expert, you will want to simply jump into Devo's Pitch.

### ◆ ◆ Experts Only Terrain

Brian Head is not without its extreme terrain. Topflight skiers and snowboarders have a few options on a visit to this resort. First, the real hardcore people can take a climb to the top of Brian Head Peak. The 307-foot hike up will give you access to fresh powder and bragging rights. You can find the gate for the hike at the top of the run called Outskirts.

If you prefer less work for your expert only runs, trek over to Devo's Pitch. The runs are steep, there are a ton of trees and hazards, and the setting is great. It doesn't have quite the vertical of the peak and it's not very large either. However, it remains quite steep and very challenging.

### Cruisers

Most of the runs off the Giant Steps Triple provide the perfect spot for cruising. While the area does attract a lot of snowboarders, there is more than enough space for everyone. Both skiers and snowboarders will find Sunburst to Bear Paw a great fast run. Giant Steps is

In the photo: signs reading "The Plunge" and "Last Chance"

also a great run for the more advanced skier. All three are always groomed.

If you are over on the Roulette Triple, Hard Times is not well named as it provides a nice easy cruise and some very pretty scenery. The last bit hugs the resort boundary and can be ridden on Desbah to the bottom for a longer cruise.

## Bumps

For short jaunts on the bumps, head on over to The Dunes Triple and follow the blue run Last Chance. There are several short drops off the run and they seem to develop nice moguls. In addition, The Plunge off the same lift is a good option. These runs will not wear you down but still give you the challenge you seek.

Over on the Roulette Triple, you will find a bit longer and more challenging mogul fields. Take a look under the chair to see what has formed. There may be some nicely formed bumps on Straight Up.

▲ Brian Head has unique red rock formations.

## Trees and Steeps

Devo's Pitch is certainly one of the ideal spots to find both trees and steeps. The nice steep pitch is interspersed with large trees, rocks, and challenging cliffs. For a gentler but still challenging experience, take a ride down Dark Hollow off the Roulette Triple.

### ☺ Tips and Tricks

Over the past several years, Brian Head has experienced an infestation of the hungry bark beetle. This is a natural occurrence with which the resort and the rest of the region are dealing. The results of this are thinning forest and dead trees.

Brian Head is using this situation to make an opportunity. They continue to clear up the deadwood and make the most of the prob-

▲ Enjoy a beer out on the deck or a hot chocolate inside.

lem areas. This means they will be glading for tree runs and give you a few more options to ski.

Over time, the beetle will die out and the forest will recover. However, you may notice few trees for a time. This means the resort will be a little more open, and as such, have a bit more skiing and snowboarding.

## Powder

With an open mountain and great snowfall annually, there are many places to discover the powder. However, the most popular area is over on The Dunes Triple. Because most people do not ski or snowboard in the area and because there are a lot of options, you are more likely to find untracked snow.

Of course, the real wild folks do the hike up to the top of Brian Head Peak so they can get the big powder. The peak is only open when there is a lot of snow and after avalanche control is done. The small hut on top is an old observation point and the starting point for powder seekers.

## Snowboarding

Brian Head is an excellent resort for snowboarding. With three different terrain parks, they are really putting the work into the mountain for those wanting to tear it up. Jumps, rails, and tables are all scaled to the skill level in each park. There are also tools and workbenches for riders to fix those ever-present binding issues.

## Other Activities

Because Brian Head is its own community, it strives to give people a lot of options besides skiing. They recognize that the skiing and snowboarding are not for everyone. Thus, there are a number of other winter activities available at the resort.

With a tube park, everyone can have a blast sliding down the mountain without the need of skis or snowboards. Tubing is a popular activity at Brian Head and is offered every day. In addition, visitors can find many local vendors who provide snowmobile rentals to explore the wilderness or simply experience the exhilaration of the ride.

Nordic skiing in the area is certainly available, and with breathtaking scenery nearby, it is a great option. Brian Head offers nearly 40km of trails, and nearby at Cedar Breaks National Monument, the cross-country skier can find meadows, forests, and spectacular red rock scenery to explore.

## ☺ Tips and Tricks

Georg's Ski Shop in Brian Head has been around for more than 20 years and has all the equipment you need. The charming little shop rents skis, snowboards, and Nordic equipment. It is on the edge of town as you head toward Cedar Breaks.

# Lodging

Lodging in Brian Head is different than many other places. There is no real hotel. It is an amalgamation of privately owned condos. However, that does not mean you can't find a place to stay. In fact, the resort works closely with the different companies to ensure visitors can find a place to stay throughout the season.

It is important to book early for the best prices and to find the kind of accommodation you need. Because these places are condos, they have kitchens, varying amenities, and different designs. Not all of them have pools or hot tubs. In fact, you are far more likely to find a fridge than a telephone or Internet access.

▲ Georg's is great place to find gear and rentals and to shop.

Visitors looking for more of a hotel experience should try the Cedar Breaks Lodge. It has a bar, restaurants, and beautiful condos. In addition, you will find a large indoor pool with two hot tubs, a sauna, and steam room. Best of all, guests get indoor parking and very close access to the Navajo Peak area.

If you only want to stay for a night and need quick accommodations, the town of Parowan is not far from Brian Head and has a Day's Inn. A little farther down the road is Cedar City, which has numerous options for visitors.

## Restaurants

Brian Head's on-mountain food is simply tasty ski fare. Both lodges provide the traditional burgers, fries, and chili. A nice chicken sandwich is not out of the question either. However, if you are looking for more interesting culinary choices, you may want to try the pizza at Pizano's. It is close to the base of the Giant Steps Lodge but does get very busy at lunch.

The small community of Brian Head does support a few small restaurants and it is advisable to make dinner reservations if you feel like dining out. The community is focused on condos, and as such, most people do their own cooking. A couple of small markets can provide the materials you need for a nice dinner.

If you are in a hurry to hit the slopes but need a good breakfast before the day begins, the resort does offer breakfast at its lodges. Brian Head is also proud to let people know they are purveyors of Starbucks coffee.

# 4

# Brighton Resort

## About the Resort

Locals always seem to know the best places to hang. They are not stuck on pretentiousness or trends. They want a place they feel comfortable, enjoy, and know is always going to be good. For 70 years, the people of the Salt Lake Valley have been calling Brighton their home.

Brighton was started by a ski club back in 1936 with some wire rope and some elevator parts. Today, the resort has changed significantly but the feeling you're part of a club has not. A visit to this resort evokes a feeling of discovery. It's like you have found something special and you want to share it with your friends.

Since those early days, the resort has undergone many changes designed to make the mountain more accessible and more fun. It may have a long history but the resort certainly keeps with the times. With their four high-speed chairs, Brighton opens up the opportunities to explore everything this mountain has to offer.

## ☺ Tips and Tricks

Be certain to get to the resort early on weekends and holidays. On busy days, Brighton turns away visitors when the parking lot is full. That means you will have to either take the bus or turn around and go to another resort.

Brighton has taken to snowboarding and snowboarders have taken to Brighton. The resort sports four feature-filled parks and a half-

12601 Big Cottonwood
Canyon Road
Brighton, UT 84121

**Web:** www.skibrighton.com

**E-mail:**
info@brightonresort.com

**Main:** 801-532-4731

**Snow Report:**
801-532-4731

**Ski and Snowboard
School:** 801-532-4731

**RESORT STATISTICS**

**Peak Elevation:** 10,500 feet
(3,200 meters)

**Base Elevation:** 8,755 feet
(2,669 meters)

**Vertical Drop:** 1,745 feet
(531 meters)

**Area:** 1,050 acres
(424 hectares)

**Night Skiing and
Snowboarding:** Yes

pipe. In fact, the resort even has a separate web site dedicated just to their snowboarding features. Riders looking to really shred should not miss Brighton.

Brighton is also for skiers. Catering to all skill levels, the resort has some of Utah's best powder, great steeps, and wonderful cruisers, plus an unbelievable amount of tree skiing.

Brighton also has some of the most extensive night skiing and snowboarding available. The largest illuminated area in Utah, Brighton provides access to all its terrain parks, its half-pipe, and a large amount of the Majestic Base for skiing. People wanting to hit the mountain after work or while on a business trip to Utah can find a night skiing area larger than you might believe. In addition, the resort continues to plan how they can increase the lighted area.

If all these features and facts don't entice you to visit Brighton, why not consider its low price? Brighton is committed to keeping the resort family friendly and affordable. The resort is not fancy on its accommodations but has invested where it counts. Their fast lifts and great terrain easily explain why the locals come back again and again.

▲ Deep snow is waiting for you at Brighton.

BRIGHTON RESORT

## About the Mountain

Brighton has an interesting layout with a different L shape. Two thirds of the resort faces to the west and one third faces to the north.

While both are excellent, the landscape on each is quite different from the other. Each side has its own distinct appeal.

The Millicent area, which faces north, is popular with skiers and is home to the best powder skiing at Brighton. The landscape is open with limited tree coverage and a couple of narrow canyons on either side. The large open bowls along with the experts-only terrain make this an appealing place to lose the crowds.

The Majestic area, home to the Brighton Center, is the opposite. This westward-facing mountain is larger and densely packed with trees. You will find many narrow runs with great protection from the elements and a lot larger variety of terrain options. This part of the resort plays host to most of the snowboarders but skiers love it as well.

## ☺ Tips and Tricks

Transition between the two areas is a challenge. If you are coming from the Majestic side of the mountain, you will need to get some good speed as you take the Milly Access across. It has a lot of flat spots and pushing may be your only choice if you lose your momentum.

Crossing back over to the Majestic side of the mountain means riding high and following the Majestic Access trail back across. While the run is identified as a blue, it is a relatively gentle path and it brings you to the base of the Crest Express Quad.

BRIGHTON RESORT

▲ Brighton has been a family resort for more than 70 years.

▲ Brighton offers some of the most extensive night skiing in Utah.

Because the mountain has these two areas, the resort rarely feels crowded. Of course, each lift area can be busy. This is especially true on weekends and holidays. However, while you are taking a glide down the slopes, the numerous routes keep people comfortably spread out.

In all, Brighton feels like two mountains for the price of one. You can choose your flavor of skiing or boarding and find it. Whether you are a snowboarder and want to hang on the terrain parks or you are a powder hound seeking out a beautiful tree run, you can get what you want at Brighton.

## ● Easiest Terrain

Brighton has a great number of options for the new skier or snowboarder. Beginners will want to hang by the Explorer Double until they get stable on their boards. Once you have the confidence, take

BRIGHTON RESORT

▲ Beautiful scenery is one aspect of a great Utah vacation.

some rides up and down the Majestic Quad. Its gentle cruisers provide a nice warm-up for the day.

If you feel the need to explore more green runs, the Millicent area has a lot to explore. Canyon and Main Street will have fewer visitors and will provide some wide-open terrain to give you less people to deal with.

The Snake Creek Express Quad may have a scary name but there are a few great runs for beginners to explore. Sunshine is a beautifully groomed tree run. Deer Park and Pick 'em Up make a nice combo. There is a lot of terrain off this chair and most of it exceeds a beginner's level. However, don't let that prevent you from coming and exploring.

## ☺ Tips and Tricks

The trail map is misleading when showing Hawkeye as the only way to access Snake Creek. The run is actually quite gentle and anyone with basic turning and stopping skills should have no trouble getting to the Snake Creek Express Quad.

## ■ Intermediate Terrain

The Crest Express Quad and Snake Creek Express Quad are by far the best places for intermediate skiers to hang out and enjoy the day. There are limitless routes that can be created for the blue skier when riding these two chairs. Most of the terrain off here is nicely groomed.

If you want to challenge yourself on a powder day, head over to the Millicent area and explore Easy Out and the top of Evergreen. These have enough vertical to help you get the floating sensation but are not so steep that you will get the *fear* sensation.

A great blue route that has a lot of length and some challenge is Lone Star from the top of the Snake Creek Express Quad. This endless run takes a great path down the mountain and may challenge you physically. However, the beautiful scenery is worth the long ride.

## ◆ Advanced Terrain

Brighton is one of a small number of resorts that has a chair dedicated exclusively to advanced terrain. The Great Western Express Quad is dominated by black diamond and double black diamond skiing. Certainly there are a few blue runs, but for the most part, the whole area is tough.

Besides keeping the rabble out, having an experts only chair keeps the grooming to a minimum and allows the area to build some bumps and fine skiing and snowboarding. All the area off the chair has a different character and different challenges. Experts will want to take time to explore every bit of it.

## ◆ ◆ Experts Only Terrain

If you seek big cliffs and deep snow, look no further than the top of Millicent. Scree-Slope and Lone Pine are steep and the terrain takes some serious skill to navigate. Just past this point, out of bounds, is where professional photographers congregate to shoot magazine images and make films about extreme skiers.

Another great test of skill at Brighton is to ride Western Trail from the Great Western Express Quad and then simply drop into any of the runs directly below. Most are smoking fast, scary steep, and super challenging. Take Endless Winter for a longer workout and True Grit for a brief but exciting shot.

## Cruisers

Many of the runs off the Snake Creek Express Quad are superb cruisers. The fast ride up and the smooth ride down make this a popular area of the mountain. Sunshine is especially popular with its even and wide terrain. However, all the blue and green runs off this lift are great for cruising.

Main Street on the Millicent side of the mountain is also a great cruise with many shifts in elevation. You can achieve great speed on this well-groomed run. Or, choose one of the alternate routes down and change up the feel of the run. Main Street provides a lot of options if you are just trying to find something fun.

## Bumps

Brighton has a number of good spots to find some bumps. In fact, you have almost a menu of choices to select from while riding Elk Park Ridge off the Great Western Express Quad. Yet, there are a lot of additional options available to the person who is seeking moguls.

Ziggy and Upper Pioneer are shorter runs off the Snake Creek Express Quad that get some nicely developed smaller bumps appropriate for intermediate skiers. If you want to step up to something a little more demanding, take a peek at Wrangler.

Remember, grooming and snowfall do change the features of a mountain and Brighton gets a lot of both. If the bumps are not too deep, it could be that they recently took a cat over it. Examine the daily grooming report to see what has been worked recently. If this is the case, you could still take the run and help rebuild.

## Trees and Steeps

A majority of the Majestic area has some wonderful tree skiing. If you take a look at the side of most runs, you will see small trails popping in and out of the trees. It is a blast to weave in and out. These short visits into the trees are a great way to have fun and make a run have a different feel.

After a while, you will grow bold and seek out new trails and connect to other terrain. This presents you with a unique ride every time. These paths to discovery are a blast. Remember, if you grow

▲ Brighton is magical in the evening.

fatigued, simply exit back onto a groomed run. However, make certain to look up the hill before entering.

More advanced skiers will head off the top of the Snake Creek Express Quad and drop into Saw Buck. This steep and thick forest is only for those up to the challenge. However, its dense pines are incredible after a good snowfall.

## Powder

The Millicent area, which does not receive the amount of traffic as other areas of the resort, has Brighton's best powder. The land is wide

▲ The terrain at Brighton is perfect for beginners and powder hounds.

open and becomes a field of fresh snow after a good dump. Any path down is going to give you an amazing experience.

The real benefit of this area is that even intermediate level skiers and snowboarders can find a route down. If you are new to powder, you can find enough vertical to keep you moving but nothing too steep. Millicent is excellent for those who are still learning the fine art of skiing or snowboarding in deep snow.

Be aware that the end of the Evergreen area has a strange exit and blue riders should leave higher up. As you descend, the trail narrows and funnels into a small catwalk with a lot of dips and drops. It is challenging and will cause some people issues when trying to return to the base.

## Snowboarding

You are going to feel very special if you are a snowboarder. Brighton excels at giving snowboarders feature upon feature to jump, kick, ride, and fly over. Any one of the four terrain parks and their famous half-pipe will have you head over board in love.

At the top of the mountain is My O My, which has three large (and progressively larger) jumps. Their second park is called Candyland, a collection of rails, bars, boxes, and other implements to send you flying. Just below the half-pipe is Lower Majestic, which has a wall ride and other features. The three of these are suited to all skill levels and have features of varying degrees of difficulty.

If you are a bit more advanced, you will want to hit the Upper Majestic Park and the Half-Pipe. Upper Majestic assembles some of the more difficult features such as larger boxes, walls, and a jump they fondly call Big Bertha. At the bottom, the Half-Pipe is massive at 400 feet long with 16-foot-high walls.

### ☺ Tips and Tricks

Terrain parks are not just for snowboarders. With the advent of twin tip skis, the fine art of *hot dogging* is still alive. Brighton has instructors for both skiing and snowboarding who can help you learn the tricks of the trade.

If flying off rails and jumps just isn't your thing, then a great way to pass the time is to sit and watch. Whether it is the big air or the big crashes, the half-pipes and terrain parks are a blast to sit and watch.

### Other Activities

While Brighton does not offer cross-country skiing as part of the resort, they are close to Solitude's extensive Nordic facility. While this may seem strange to reference another resort's options here, Solitude and Brighton actually have a partnership. In fact, you can purchase a lift ticket for both resorts for one price.

The Solbright Connection is a single ticket purchase that allows you to ski between Solitude and Brighton during a single day. If you are feeling the need to ski two resorts instead of one, you can double the amount of terrain available to you. A simple trail exists between the two resorts so you can easily enjoy both with little effort.

## Lodging

Brighton does have a small lodge at the base of the resort. The accommodations reflect Brighton's sensible charm and are nothing fancy. They offer comfortable interiors and a nice place to stay. Just like the rest of Brighton, it feels like you are visiting with some friends.

Most people stay in the Salt Lake City area. It has a large assortment of choices and downtown is only 30 minutes from the resort base. In fact, many people will simply find a nice hotel in the city and rent a car to get to Brighton. However, Utah has a top notch transit system and you can actually ride a bus to the resort.

## Restaurants

Brighton actually has some surprising little tricks for getting great food. Over at the base you will find standard ski fare at the Alpine Rose, a cafeteria-style restaurant. However, if you crave something more interesting, take a walk over to Molly Green's, a full-service restaurant and private club.

Molly's is the perfect place to hang out at Brighton. It reeks of local color and personality, complete with neon beer signs and rustic bar interior. If you are over 21, stop in for a fantastic lunch or for a beer after your last run. The food and service are both excellent.

## ☺ Tips and Tricks

Lunch early or late if you are planning on hitting Molly Green's on a weekend or during a holiday. The place is not very big and gets crowded very quickly.

Brighton also offers food service at the base of the Millicent area. While the food is simple, reputation states that they make a mean breakfast burrito. In all, it is a good place to catch that morning cup of coffee before sinking deep in some fresh white snow.

# 5

# The Canyons

## About the Resort

You can certainly find something unique about each resort in Utah. They all have distinctive aspects that separate them from one another. Whether it is the great powder, unsurpassed food, or best snowboarding, each strives to be unique. However, of all the resorts in the state, the most distinctive must be The Canyons.

While the area is the newest of the three Park City resorts, it actually has been around for a long time. Originally known as Park West, it has undergone a huge transformation since it had that name. Previous visitors may think they know the resort but the changes have been significant.

The Canyons is five distinct ski areas encompassed into a single resort. Its unique topography and variety of offerings separates it from many of the other mountains in Utah. If you want to get a taste of everything in one single resort, The Canyons might be your best choice.

Each of its areas provides a unique component of snowboarding and skiing. From delicate glades of trees to open bowl skiing, The Canyons has it all. Their five different areas feel like a menu of choices where you get to select your favorite. With this kind of variety, a visitor could get spoiled at The Canyons.

Trying to provide their visitor with the entire vacation experience, The Canyons has developed a large area at the base of the resort that hosts a large variety of shops, restaurants, and bars, plus their beautiful new lodges. They host concerts and special events and have worked hard to make their base area a hub of activity.

4000 The Canyons Resort
 Drive
Park City, UT 84098
**Web:** www.thecanyons.com
**E-mail:** info@the
 canyons.com
**Main:** 435-649-5400
**Snow Report:**
 435-615-3456
**Ski and Snowboard
 School:** 435-649-5400
**RESORT STATISTICS**
**Peak Elevation:** 9,990 feet
 (3,044 meters)
**Base Elevation:** 6,800 feet
 (2,072 meters)
**Vertical Drop:** 3,190 feet
 (972 meters)
**Area:** 3,700 acres
 (1,497 hectares)
**Night Skiing and
 Snowboarding:** No

▲ The Canyons is an enormous resort with something for everyone.

In all, The Canyons provides its guests with the complete ski vacation. A large mountain, great variety of terrain, vibrant base area activities, and amazing mountainside hotels are all part of the experience. If you are seeking all the elements for a unique vacation experience, look no further than The Canyons.

## About the Mountain

The Canyons' name is not simply window dressing. It is a series of eight peaks and a multitude of canyons crossing a massive 3,700 acres, making it one of the largest resorts in Utah. With this much terrain, only your imagination is the limit on the kind of skiing and snowboarding you want to undertake.

The Canyons is not without its challenges. Trekking across the mountain does take some time and you will need to take several lifts

▲ Catch some air at The Canyons.

to enjoy it all. However, the best part of experiencing this resort is the journey. As you move from canyon to canyon, the resort transforms into different types of skiing and snowboarding.

Each area at The Canyons is like a mini resort within a greater whole package. From the beautiful tree skiing and powder on Dreamcatcher to the frightening fast cruisers off the Super Condor area, you really can get a bit of everything here.

Beginning the day at The Canyons takes at least one, if not two rides. If you drive in, you have to ride the Cabriolet. This standing

▲ The Gondola at The Canyons transports you to the heart of the resort.

ski lift transports you from the parking lot to the base area. Only guests in The Canyons lodging can park at the base of the mountain. From there, you take The Flight of The Canyons Gondola.

## ☺ Tips and Tricks

Get to the resort early and leave early. The crowds heading up the mountain have a tendency to get backed up in morning when people are trying to get on the slopes. If you are late and the line is too long, hike up the hill above the Gondola and take the Golden Eagle Double. This will definitely get you on the mountain faster.

On the way out, many people opt to take the Gondola rather than ski down. The lines at the Gondola and Short Cut Triple can get long if you wait until the last moment. If you plan properly, spend your late afternoon over on the Golden Eagle Double to get in the last run.

Once on the mountain, your options open up. The Red Pine area has two lifts servicing the base. You can also take a nice ride down Chicane to the Tombstone Six-Pack. This high-speed chair is centrally located to give you access to either side of the mountain. To the right brings you back to Red Pine, while to your left you can head to Ninety-Nine 90.

Ninety-Nine 90 is one of the experts only areas of the mountain. It features the highest slopes and the best powder at The Canyons. There is gate access on this area of the mountain if you want to do some chutes or are looking for some seriously steep terrain. If you decide this is a little too much, hop on the Peak 5 Quad and take it to the Dreamscape Quad.

Over on Dream Peak you will find some beautiful cruisers and access to some of the loveliest skiing on the mountain. Aspens and pines decorate your path as you cruise through beautifully groomed slopes. This area's name really does describe the terrain.

## ☺ Tips and Tricks

The Day Break Triple services residents of The Colony. The exclusive homes located in this mountain community use the lift for resort access. Unless you are shopping for real estate, the lift ride is a waste of time.

The Dreamcatcher Quad services an area left ungroomed and untamed for the more advanced skier and snowboarder. Trees and deep snow reside in this untouched part of the mountain. Experts congregate here for some fine fresh powder and glades.

On the opposite side of the mountain are the Saddleback Triple and Sun Peak Express Quad. These areas are popular spots for snowboarding as it is the location for both of their terrain parks. However, skiers will find the wide-open runs and great cruisers a lot of fun as well.

Last is the Super Condor area of the resort. The skiing and snowboarding here is for advanced and experts only. The skilled rider will find a variety of steeps and trees to explore as well as some brilliant cruisers. This area of the mountain gets very few of the crowds and is sort of a haven on busy days.

The Canyons has a lot to offer its visitors. It feels more like five separate resorts contained within one immense interconnecting tour than a single resort. Offering tremendous variety and beautiful landscape, The Canyons is an epic adventure waiting for you.

## ● Easiest Terrain

Of all the resorts in Utah, The Canyons has the smallest collection of easiest runs. They simply don't offer a lot of choices to beginning skiers and snowboarders. So, when you start to scan the trail map for green runs, don't be surprised that only 14 percent of this resort is actually rated as easiest.

The learning area of the mountain is located off the High Meadow Quad. If you are new to skiing or snowboarding, you will have to ride The Flight of The Canyons Gondola up and back. Riding a gondola is easy. It's like riding a bus. Carry your skis up to the door, hand them to one of the operators, and sit down inside.

Other than the few runs off the High Meadow Quad, there is the Sunrise Double at the very base, which accesses a few other runs. Simply stated, beginning skiers and snowboarders don't really have a ton of choices. However, many of the intermediate areas on the mountain are very nice and it won't be long before you can handle it.

## ■ Intermediate Terrain

There are tons of options for intermediate skiers and snowboarders at The Canyons. In fact, there are so many great choices that you may struggle with where to start. However, the one real benefit is that you can pick an area to explore and stay there for several hours before feeling like you really tried it all. Then move on to the next area.

By far, the best area of the mountain for intermediates is the Dreamscape Quad. All of the blue terrain on that side of the resort is nicely groomed, great for cruising, and really beautiful. The entire area accessed by the lift is exclusively blue so you can't make a wrong choice. In addition, because it takes two chair rides to get there, the crowds are light.

The Tombstone Express Six-Pack area has some great runs but it is a mix of blue and black. Traffic can get a little heavy on the lift because it is a key connector to both sides of the resort. However, most people don't ski the great runs below as they are moving on to other areas of the mountain. Try Cloud 9 or Another World for a great experience.

The Canyons also features some double blue runs. These are for advanced intermediates who want a few more steeps, bumps, and drops. The Super Condor Express Quad is an excellent spot to test

▲ The Canyons provides wide open terrain—a snowboarder's delight.

▲ Ski over roads and under bridges as you traverse through
The Colony at The Canyons.

your skills. The runs are fast and fun. Aplande and Kestrel are great on the vertical, and check out Canis Lupis for a sweet natural half-pipe.

### ◆ Advanced Terrain

The Canyons provides abundant choices for the expert skier. The whole mountain is covered with a variety of black diamond runs, and with only one or two exceptions, a person can literally pick a lift and find an expert run to explore.

With these vast options, it is hard to direct anyone to one particular spot on the mountain for the best terrain. However, there are certain hot spots that seem to attract skiers and snowboarders. Experts seem to congregate at the Ninety-Nine 90 area and Saddleback. Both have excellent skiing, but you can find less crowded and equally good terrain on other spots around the mountain.

The Dreamcatcher Quad is an area of The Canyons that remains untouched by snowcats and the resort. It is just one large tree area with some runs carefully cut through the forest. You will find this area a challenging yet serene spot for expert skiing.

Because of its outlying position on the mountain, the Super Condor Express gets fewer skiers but has some great long runs with varying degrees of difficulty. Take the Apex Ridge across. On the right, the runs are short, steep, and bumpy. On the left, you will find long, drawn-out fields of bumps and edge-riding steeps.

### ◆ ◆ Experts Only Terrain

If you want lift-accessible skiing without a hike, there is one spot that everyone needs to visit at The Canyons and it is Ninety-Nine 90. When the snow is deep, it is certainly one of the best areas on the mountain. You won't feel right if you don't make a visit to this area. Some of the best skiing is straight down Fright Gully and Dutch Hollow.

### ☺ Tips and Tricks

One spot that is great for your vanity and will impress your friends and family is to take the intermediate skiers to the Saddleback Express Quad and let them take down Kokopelli to Main Line. Then, ride Elk Ridge above them and drop in on Shadows, Gallery, or Ecstasy. As they look up, they will see you in all your glory. Don't biff it!

▲ The Canyons has great in-bounds backcountry-type skiing.

If you feel like hiking, the resort even grows bigger. Murdock Bowl and Redpine Bowl will fulfill those steep and deep desires. Great vertical and largely ignored by most of the visitors to the resort, these two areas have extreme written all over them. You will need to check to see if they have enough snow and are open before venturing upward.

## Cruisers

The Dreamscape Quad is not simply appealing because of its nicely flowing gentle terrain. The entire area is possibly the best cruising on the mountain. There are some great runs elsewhere, but you will not find a larger collection off a single chair anywhere else.

The area is called Snow Meadow and it is a delight. With a virtual buffet of cruisers, you can mix and match until you find the perfect run. The bottom runs through The Colony, a luxury home area at the resort. It is sort of fun to ski under their bridges and over roads as you approach the lift.

Boa, off the Super Condor Express Quad, is one for the books. It is really long and really fast. You will find yourself involuntarily screaming as you fly down this wide and long speed machine. It is a fun cruise at any speed, but you can really get moving if you want.

## Bumps

The Tombstone Express Quad is a great vantage point for checking out some of the best bump runs at The Canyons. Beneath the lift you will find Thunder and Lightning dropping into the gully. On the opposite side, the Paradise Chutes keep you on your edge and really test the fall line.

If you are still working on the bumps and need a little practice, head over to Mine Shaft off the Sun Peak Express Quad. The moguls form below the chair and are nicely formed. There isn't a huge amount of vertical, but the terrain will still give you a nice challenge to find that rhythm.

## Trees and Steeps

Skiing in nicely cut glades and dropping down chutes are two of best things about The Canyons. There are hundreds of spots around the mountain that will give you the thrill and exhilaration of fresh snow, steep drops, and carving turns in a forest. Even better, they are all really accessible.

For trees, the Abyss off the Peak 5 Quad, The Pines off the Saddleback Express, and literally anything on the Dreamcatcher Quad will answer the need for glade skiing. These areas have varying degrees of pitch and are great when the snow is really deep.

## Powder

You can certainly find a lot of the fresh white stuff at The Canyons, as you can at all the Utah resorts. However, the tremendous size of the resort does mean that you will have better luck finding more of it uncut and less tracked out.

Any of the upper mountain lifts are going to be the key destinations for powder hounds. Thus, you may want to try your luck at some of the lower lifts or head to the edges of the resort. The more popular spots are well known and will fill fast.

Try the gates at the top of the Tombstone Express Six-Pack. Deshutes or Grande may be good choices. Of course, the multi-lift ride to the Dreamcatcher Quad will dissuade the more eager powder seekers. And last, the Super Condor Express will also see less traffic.

## Snowboarding

Snowboarders will be pleased. The terrain parks at The Canyons are not only easy to access, but they are close to one another and offer some great features. You can access the big jumps, walls, and rails off the Sun Peak Express Quad on Upper and Lower Respect. There is a smaller park for learning up at the top of Painted Horse, accessible from the Saddleback Express Quad.

While the resort does not have a half-pipe, it does have six natural half-pipes, which are well maintained and fun for boarders to explore. In fact, The Canyons features these spots on their trail map and encourage riders to give each a try.

## Lodging

Millions of dollars have been invested into The Canyons over the last several years. They have grown and built to make this a world-class destination. The resort has three hotels with every amenity. The Sundial, Grand Summit, and Silverado Lodges provide a variety of options for vacationers.

The Sundial Lodge is a hotel with condominium-style rooms, the Grand Summit is a traditional hotel but with every feature you can imagine, and the Silverado Lodge is a condominium development. All three allow you to enjoy the resort without the need of a car. Walk out the door to ski, shop, or dine.

In addition, Park City is very close, and if you don't want to stay on mountain, there are innumerable choices for lodging in the area. In fact, the terrific shuttle services, taxis, and other transportation options in the Park City area make staying anywhere in the valley convenient and easy for all three resorts.

## Restaurants

The Canyons has a great selection of restaurants on and at the base of the mountain. The best thing is all of them are good. Their cafeterias provide more choices than a lot of other ski resorts. Burgers and fries are there, but a nice turkey sandwich with pesto is also an option.

Red Pine Lodge is by far the most popular place because of its location and it is pretty good. It is especially nice on a beautiful day because of its large outdoor seating area. Lookout Cabin is a nicer option if you want to sit, relax, and enjoy the food. Last, the Sun Lodge is designed to lure the crowds away from Red Pine with superior food.

### ☺ Tips and Tricks

The Red Pine Lodge is a zoo at lunchtime. The crowds make it impossible to find a place to sit and eat. If you really crave a regular cafeteria-style lunch, either eat early or after 1 PM. Otherwise, avoid it entirely and try any of the other mountain restaurants. They are all excellent!

Another good option is to simply ski to the base and have lunch at one of the several restaurants and bars located in the village. There is every option from a quick bite to full-service dining. Once you are done, hop on the Gondola and get back to the fun.

# 6

# Deer Valley Resort

## About the Resort

There are those who aspire to perfection and those who actually achieve it. It takes balance, skill, and understanding to successfully bring a variety of complex elements together to make something perfect. Yet, there is a place where perfection happens every day and that place is Deer Valley.

Deer Valley Resort has been giving skiers one wonderful season after another through the attention to details. From carrying skis from your car to the ticket window to having bathrooms at the base and top of most lifts, they think about not only what people want but also what people need.

Deer Valley cares about you. They restrict the number of skiers so you don't have to wait in long lift lines. They groom constantly so you won't have an unexpected bump or rough snow. They provide five-star dining at all levels of the resort so that chocolate chip cookie is as good as that tiramisu. They do it all for you.

## ☺ Tips and Tricks

Deer Valley controls the sales of lift tickets to ensure lift lines stay comfortably sized. If you are visiting during a busy holiday period, you will want to buy your tickets in advance. Also, if you plan on putting your kids in ski school, make a reservation. It fills up fast.

Throughout the past 25 years, Deer Valley has been consistently named as one of the top resorts in North America (if not *the* top).

P.O. Box 1525
Park City, UT 84060
**Web:** www.deervalley.com
**E-mail:** marketing@
deervalley.com
**Main:** 435-649-1000
**Snow Report:**
435-649-2000
**Ski School:** 435-649-6648
**RESORT STATISTICS**
**Peak Elevation:** 9,570 feet
(2,916 meters)
**Base Elevation:** 6,570 feet
(2,002 meters)
**Vertical Drop:** 3,000 feet
(914 meters)
**Area:** 1,750 acres
(708 hectares)
**Night Skiing:** No

They earn these awards because they continue to strive to make their resort the best in the world. This is not simply about the amenities and the customer service. It's about everything.

The rich and famous flock here because it is unsurpassed. They come for the spectacular terrain, incredible scenery and the posh treatment. However, the greatest thing about Deer Valley is they treat everyone like they are a celebrity. Those of us who pay mortgages and have regular lives feel like stars when we visit this fantastic resort.

Some people question whether Deer Valley is worth paying a premium price. There is a perception that there is too much here and the resort doesn't cater to real skiers. I have to disagree. I wonder how much you are willing to pay for perfection. Deer Valley is a value at any price.

DEER VALLEY RESORT

▲ Deer Valley has great untracked powder just waiting to be explored.

## About the Mountain

There has been a long running perception that the skiing at Deer Valley is strictly for beginners and intermediates that ski groomed runs. Certainly, this is the hallmark of what has made the resort famous. However, there is much more to this mountain and there is something for everyone of every level.

Deer Valley has three lodges and two separate base areas. The Snow Park Lodge is the main base where most visitors start their day. However, Silver Lake Lodge is another large base. Destination skiers who are staying in the surrounding village or at the famous Stein

▲ Mountain hosts are just one of the many services at Deer Valley.

Eriksen Lodge begin their ski day here. Last, the newest lodge is Empire Canyon.

## ☺ Tips and Tricks

Yes, those people are really carrying your skis! Parking at Deer Valley might be confusing for first-time visitors. If you are driving in for the day, head to the Snow Park Lodge and drive around to the front of the resort. The people there will unload your gear, allow you to drop off any family or friends, and then park your car.

You will quickly discover that Deer Valley is a very large resort. Spread out across five different peaks, each mountain has its own distinctive type of skiing. Still, other than Empire Canyon, every mountain has a green route down and you will find all levels of skiing across the entire resort.

In fact, Deer Valley has gone to the trouble to include all levels of skiing on each mountain so families and friends can ski together.

DEER VALLEY RESORT

▲ Deer Valley limits the number of skiers so you can really enjoy your day.

In most cases, skiers of varying skills can start in the same place and then divert only to meet up a short time later. This convenience is simply another thoughtful aspect of this beautiful resort.

The Little Baldy Peak is the quiet spot at the resort. A lot of people aren't aware it exists, and while it is smaller, there are some fun and interesting choices to explore. Blue skiers can ride the Jordanelle Gondola in comfort. It is especially nice on bad weather days.

## ☺ Tips and Tricks

The Jordanelle Base is accessed from US 40 and services people coming from the Heber Valley. However, if you want to avoid the main resort and just get right to skiing, you can park and purchase your lift ticket here.

Bald Eagle Mountain is the central peak of the resort. It provides access to Silver Lake and is where skiers at Snow Park get their start. Skiing here is predominantly for intermediates. You will also find the ski school at the base.

Flagstaff Mountain is by far the best blue skiing at the resort. A significant portion of the mountain is dedicated to intermediates and the terrain is beautiful. You will find perfectly groomed terrain with a nice pitch and great scenery on every run.

Advanced and expert skiers are going to head up to Bald Mountain or Empire Canyon. Both have a large collection of black diamond terrain. Bumps, chutes, steeps, and tree skiing are all featured on these peaks.

One thing to be aware of is that Deer Valley does not allow snowboarding. While the management at the resort has no issue with the sport, they have chosen to listen to their customers. The overwhelming support to make this resort *skiers only* has kept boarders off the slope.

If your family has a mix of snowboarders and skiers, simply grab a bus. The Park City bus system is excellent and a quick ride over to one of the other two area resorts is very easy. Also, many of the local lodges will help you with transportation. Both the Canyons and Park City have excellent amenities for snowboarders.

Deer Valley's terrain is as diverse as it is refined. You can find the best of everything here. The mountain offers terrain for all level of skiers, so whether you are taking your first tracks ever or you are running the chutes, you can find the kind of skiing you want.

## ● Easiest Terrain

Among all the resorts in Utah, Deer Valley caters the most to those who are new on skis. Their incredible grooming and the accessibility to green runs make it one of the most inviting resorts in the world. A novice can easily find several comfortable options to explore as he or she starts on skis.

## ☺ Tips and Tricks

At the top of every lift at Deer Valley, there are two amenities that make life wonderful for every new visitor. First, you will find a mountain host there to help you find your way down. These friendly people know the mountain well and can help you make the most of every trip up and down the lift.

▲ Deer Valley impeccably grooms its trails.

Next, there is a bathroom at the top or bottom of every lift. You will not have to make an embarrassing stop in the woods if you need an important break. In addition, Deer Valley's ski patrol huts do not have the amenities of the lodges but are great places to warm up if you are really cold. They even have dryers for those soaked gloves and hats.

There is a green run from the top of every chairlift with the exception of the Empire Canyon Quad. This means that you can explore the entire mountain without feeling like some of it is out of reach. Watch the crazies jump into a chute or scope out some massive bumps and still have a nice ride down.

New visitors to Deer Valley may want to hop on the Carpenter Express Quad and begin with Success. The run has a very smooth pitch and is the perfect length for beginners to stretch out the legs. In addition, there are some gentle blues just off the run for when you start to get some confidence.

▲ Deep snow and a picture-perfect landscape make Deer Valley a popular destination.

While Deer Valley regulates the number of skiers, you can find isolation on the Deer Crest Quad. Deer Hollow is a nice long run that rarely gets any traffic. Most people do not ski the area and you will be able to experience the beauty of Deer Valley with a feeling of privacy.

## ■ Intermediate Terrain

Deer Valley is heaven for intermediate skiers. Most people who choose Deer Valley as a destination profile themselves as intermediate level skiers, and the resort has listened. Their exquisite grooming and well-managed terrain are perfectly suited for this level of skier.

The resort offers all types of terrain but it is renowned for its blue skiing. Not only is half the resort dedicated to blue runs, there is one located at the top of every lift. That means the intermediate skier can ski anywhere on the mountain and find a comfortable way down.

A grooming report is a great way to find out which runs are going to be easier for new intermediates. Blue pistes aren't always groomed. Grab the report from the lodge or at the ticket office and you can see what has had some maintenance since the last snow. It will ensure you have a nice ride down.

If you don't want to waste any time, head straight to Flagstaff Mountain and explore any of the runs in that area. Blue Bell and Hawkeye are great choices. However, all the runs here will give you a comfortable place to start your day.

After the warm-ups, hit Bald Mountain and take Tycoon for a long fun ride down to the Sultan Express Quad. At the top of the lift, Stein's Way is well known for great speed and a lot of fun. There is a black portion so be certain to hop over to Perseverance to divert. However, this may be your chance to move to next level.

Intermediate skiers still trying to perfect their skills may want to avoid Bald Mountain and Empire Canyon. The intermediate runs in these areas are a touch steeper and are not as easy as some of the other parts of the mountain.

## ◆ Advanced Terrain

Bald Mountain has the greatest number of advanced runs and is where experts head when they want some hard work. There are many routes down that will test your ability and your strength. Long stretches of bumps are not uncommon and the steeps have a fierce pitch.

Empire Canyon is more like backcountry and bowl skiing. Open terrain with great steeps can be accessed directly off the lift. If you are ready for some traversing and possibly some hiking, you can follow the ridgeline.

## ◆ ◆ Experts Only Terrain

Empire Canyon and the Daly Chutes are just what you need to get the adrenaline pumping. Steep and deep, they are straight shots down and loads of fun. Stay high off the Empire Express Quad and then keep your speed as you traverse the top. The skiing here is extreme and extremely fun.

Over on Bald Mountain, Mayflower Bowl gets some wonderful snow and you can be certain to find some fresh powder. That whole

▲ The Beach is a popular hang-out spot to catch some sun.

backside of Bald Mountain is challenging skiing, and while it may not have a double black on each run, the bumps are big and the terrain is steep.

## Cruisers

There are so many options for cruisers at Deer Valley that it may be impossible to select one that stands out. The resort prides itself on keeping its customers happy with the perfect conditions for cruising on most of the mountain. Corduroy terrain and wide-open space are Deer Valley trademarks.

### ☺ Tips and Tricks

One favorite that many people enjoy is taking Last Chance off the Carpenter Quad or Silver Lake Quad. The run is not about the skiing but rather the scenery. Decorating the homes along the route is a variety of different sculptures.

▶ Deep snow and glade skiing are part of the Deer Valley experience.

Styles of the sculptures range from artistic to comic, and they are something to see. The kids will love the bear family or the crazy raccoons. You will definitely want to take one or two turns down this one and bring your camera.

The Little Baldy area is perfect if you are looking for quiet cruising. Jordanelle is an excellent long run with a great pitch. You get a lot of speed and feel your thighs burning if you take it top to bottom.

Of course anything on Flagstaff is going to keep you cruising. However, if you want to step up your speed, move over to Keno and then make a cut over to Nabob off the Sterling Express Quad. The runs off this chair all have a nice pitch and get you really moving.

## Bumps

If you want to work out where the pros test their skills, head over to the bottom of Snow Park. The FIS Freestyle Championships were held here in 2003 and will be held again in 2011. The international community has embraced Deer Valley as a key location for aerial and mogul skiing since hosting the events during the 2002 Winter Olympics.

White Owl, Champion, and Lucky Bill all have terrain where the resort forms and builds monsters. The bumps resemble boulders and are perfectly spaced for the pros to slam their knees. However, they may be closed to the public if an event is coming up.

Other good choices include Narrow Gauge off the Mayflower Triple or Square Deal over on the Quincy Express Quad. If you are an aspiring bump runner, try Lost Boulder for manageable-sized moguls.

## Trees and Steeps

As with everything at Deer Valley, tree skiing is well done. You will find delicately designed glades to get into the forest and find that fresh snow. Triangle Trees rides directly below Tycoon and flows down nicely to the Sultan Connection. It is a great spot after a dump of powder.

If you are at the top of Bald Mountain after riding the Sultan Express Quad, follow the green run called Homeward Bound over to the top of Sunset Glade. The tree skiing here is wondrous and the run has a more delicate pitch. You will find excellent spacing and comfortable pace through the aspens.

Steep pitches can be found over on the Mayflower Triple and the Sultan Express Quad. You may want to explore Rattler but it does get bumped up. Also in that area, the Mayflower Chutes are likely to make you weak in the knees.

## Powder

There is a little known fact that a lot of the best untracked powder can be found at Deer Valley. A vast majority of the visitors to this beautiful resort are destination skiers who are focused on skiing groomed runs. These people have little experience with Utah's fresh snow and prefer to keep to the easier and more comfortable runs.

After a good dump of snow, the resort is a literal treasure trove of powder spots. Even days after the snow has fallen, many places

► Deer Valley is world renowned for its gourmet dining.

DEER VALLEY RESORT

on the mountain still have untracked powder. While the more popular powder destinations are being tracked out, you can be certain Deer Valley will still have a spot for you.

Some of the best known holes are Lady Morgan Bowl off the Empire Express Quad and Mayflower Bowl off the Mayflower Triple. However, what most people don't know about is the Ontario Bowl over on Flagstaff. Take the Quincy Express Quad and ride Ontario for a short jaunt and then follow the traverse.

## Lodging

Deer Valley does not own their own lodging but you need not look far to see their name all over a number of top quality resorts. They closely associate themselves with many of the condominium and hotel developments to ensure they meet their exacting standard. Thus, you will find the same level of service and commitment.

Of these, the premier resort is the Stein Eriksen Lodge. While not owned by the legendary skier, his medals and trophies can be viewed in the lobby, and the lodge retains his Norwegian heritage in its design. The service and food are impeccable and offer ski-in and ski-out convenience. Even if you don't choose to stay here, you really ought to drop in for brunch or dinner.

Deer Valley does provide a central reservation system to ensure you get accommodations that meet your needs and their standards. However, Park City is very close and you can find a host of other choices available to you that are going to be very nice.

## Restaurants

Where do you start when talking about dining at Deer Valley? The resort is renowned for its incredible food, luxuriant lodges, and outstanding service. All three combine to provide the perfect dining experience. Here you have the epitome of mountain dining.

Deer Valley is famous for its food. It broke the mold years ago by destroying the conceived notions of what skiers should eat. The standard burger fries or chili were not thrown out entirely but classed up and given a whole new perspective. Their turkey chili is legendary and worth trying at least once.

If you don't want cafeteria-style dining, the resort does offer sit-down dining options at most of their lodges. For example, the Royal Street Café has wonderful food and is easy to access in the Silver Lake Lodge. While reservations aren't necessary, they are recommended.

# Park City Mountain Resort

## About the Resort

There are few resorts in Utah that have the reputation or celebrity of Park City. Home to the Sundance Film Festival and the haunt of celebrities throughout the winter months, the resort is certainly one of Utah's most popular destinations. However, Park City has earned this distinction. It is a first-rate resort surrounded by a charming town.

Founded by miners in the late 19th century, Park City was a town built out of silver. Ex-army and rail employees moved to the small mountain village to seek their fortune. Sadly, the price of silver depreciated over time, and by the 1950s, most mining operations shut down. However, clever entrepreneurs decided to use the old mine cars and rail systems to introduce the growing sport of skiing.

Contemporary Park City still holds the allure of its past and strives to maintain that character. Main Street is decorated with many of the original structures from its mining heyday. In addition, new structures are built to maintain the appearance of the original town. Visitors feel like they have stepped into the past while walking its streets.

As you traverse its slopes, Park City Mountain Resort also transports you to the past. You can see evidence of its mining history all over the mountain. Large implements, buildings, and structures decorate the resort and add a fascinating historical perspective to your skiing and snowboarding vacation.

1310 Lowell Avenue
Park City, UT 84060

**Web:** www.parkcity
mountain.com

**E-mail:** info@pcski.com

**Main:** 435-649-8111

**Snow Report:**
435-647-5449

**Ski and Snowboard
School:** 435-658-5560

**RESORT STATISTICS**

**Peak Elevation:**
10,000 feet
(3,048 meters)

**Base Elevation:** 6,900 feet
(2,103 meters)

**Vertical Drop:** 3,100 feet
(945 meters)

**Area:** 3,300 acres
(1,335 hectares)

**Night Skiing and
Snowboarding:** Yes

▲ Take a ride on the wild side on one of Park City's multiple riding features.

## ☺ Tips and Tricks

If you are fascinated by the mining history of Park City, seek out the pick axe icon on the trail map for points of interest. These are informative plaques located around the mountain.

However, Park City is certainly not without modern amenities. The town and resort are thriving with elegant restaurants, fashionable boutiques, and great accommodations. They have installed a large collection of high-speed, six-pack lifts to ensure lift lines are small, and they have specialized their grooming to ensure you get the best runs possible.

All the elements of a great winter vacation come together in Park City. Whether strolling down the historic main street in the evening or riding a high-speed chair to a terrain park, Park City brings together the best of the old and the new to create one of Utah's best destinations.

## About the Mountain

Park City is a large resort. In fact, it is one of Utah's biggest. It has four different areas serviced by 17 different lifts. However, this large size is very well planned and easy to navigate. In fact, lift placement is so good that you could be at the furthest reaches of the resort and return to the base riding only one lift.

This convenience translates into two significant benefits. First, the runs at Park City are as long as you want them to be. If you want, you could ski or snowboard miles in a single day. Next, you can explore a wide mixture of terrain without having to traverse numerous lifts. The well-placed chairs open up the mountain to a multitude of options.

Mountain access is straightforward and there are many ways to find wonderful skiing and snowboarding quickly. Everything starts at the Resort Center and then goes up from there. Park City's amazing infrastructure supports thousands of riders. They have placed high-speed quads and six-packs across the mountain, ensuring small lift lines and more slope time.

Park City has also planned the mountain so people can find their interest in most areas without having to traverse the whole resort. For example, you will come across many lifts that serve both intermediate and experts. There are a few exceptions, but in the end, friends or family of varying skill levels can enjoy the resort together.

Park City also gives you the best information. From the extensive grooming reports to the friendly mountain hosts, it strives to

▶ Even as large as Park City is, one can find serene spots to enjoy.

take the guesswork out of visiting. All of this is aimed toward a common goal. Ultimately, Park City gives you more of everything—more rides, more opportunities, more information, more terrain, and most importantly, more fun.

### ● Easiest Terrain

From the base of the mountain, Park City provides two lifts to ease beginning skiers and snowboarders into their sports. The First Time Quad and the Three Kings Double are both short and only service green runs. The First Time has a focus on skiing, while the Three Kings Double has a beginner terrain park.

Once you have gained a bit of confidence, you can take a ride on the Payday Six-Pack. There are only a few easy runs down from the top, but as your skills improve, you can explore other gentle green runs. Homerun is the safe bet to take you to the base.

### ☺ Tips and Tricks

▲ Snowboarders have a lot of options at Park City.

One of the most common ways down the mountain at the end of the day is the Gotcha Cut-Off and it is simply miserable. It is overused and icy. Plan your day out so you end up on Homerun or over toward the Payday Six-Pack.

More advanced green skiers can ride the Bonanza Six-Pack and ski off the Pioneer Triple. There are a few more green options off that lift, and when you are done, you can simply hop on Homerun to get you back to the Resort Center.

### ■ Intermediate Terrain

Until a few years ago, Park City was considered an intermediate mountain. This is because there is an amazing amount of blue terrain available. Park City has added a lot of expert terrain, but they did not decrease the quantity of intermediate skiing and snowboarding.

▲ Bumps, steeps and everything in between are available at Park City.

Mornings are great on the Silverlode Six-Pack where you can find many fun blue runs that are nicely groomed and perfect for exploring your skills. The lift serves some smooth and progressively challenging blue runs. A little bit of bumps and some steep are mingled nicely with some easy cruising.

## ☺ Tips and Tricks

Here is a great way to warm up for the day. Ride Homerun to Claim Jumper, work your way back to Assessment and Hidden Splendor, and then finish with Mel's. Mel's Alley is particularly fun with a small bit of steep at the bottom to get the blood pumping.

▲ Park City offers a wide range of perfectly groomed runs for everyone's taste.

The King Con chair is paradise for the intermediate skier or snowboarder. With 14 different blue and double blue runs, you can spend an entire day carving and coasting in comfort. To boot, you can easily access the rest of the mountain if you grow weary of all the great choices.

There are a variety of other spots on the mountain with blue runs. In fact, Park City gives you a blue route down every lift except over in Jupiter Bowl. Thus, you should certainly explore everything the resort has to offer. You may only have a couple of selections, but in the end, you will get to see more of the resort and its beautiful scenery.

## ☺ Tips and Tricks

Want to avoid lift lines in the morning rush and go straight to King Con? Slide over to the Eagle Lift. It is rarely ridden and it places you right on the top of the King Con ridgeline.

## ◆ Advanced Terrain

As with the intermediate terrain, you can also find black diamond runs off almost every lift at Park City. Thus, the advanced skier will find a lot of diverse options at Park City. Unlike most of the resorts, Park City has double blue and black skiing. This means that there are various runs offering a range of difficulty.

Resorts rate their own runs. Park City has opted to further define difficulty levels on some of their slopes. A double blue run may actually require the same skills as a black diamond run but may just have fewer elements. Unless you are really an advanced intermediate to expert skier, you may want to avoid the double blue runs.

A great place to start with a nice mix of double blue and black is over on the McConkey's Six-Pack and the Pioneer Triple. Both pro-

▲ Jupiter Bowl at Park City is legendary for its steeps.

vide lots of great skiing and boarding with nice mixes of bumps, steeps, and difficulty. This means you can shift from difficult to expert to nasty with a couple quick route changes.

Next, the Ski Team Double has some of the best steeps and bumps on the mountain, but they are rarely visited. Most people head up the mountain and pass these lower runs. They are located off an older lift and are not as accessible as some of the other terrain. However, there are some awesome steeps off this lift.

Last, the Thaynes Double is home to the biggest and baddest bumps at Park City. All the expert skiing off this lift is long and challenging. You can also take Motherload Triple if you want to get access to a few different runs in the same area. Both drop you at the bottom of Thaynes Canyon.

▲ Park City is one of America's best ski towns.

### ◆ ◆ Experts Only Terrain

Jupiter Bowl and McConkey's Bowl will have any extreme skier drooling with expectation. Jupiter is legendary for its double blacks and McConkey's offers the best glading on the mountain. Both have the steeps, trees, and chutes that experts crave. These two bowls are certainly worthy challenges for any expert skier.

Jupiter serves exclusively double black terrain and holds some of the finest in-bounds backcountry skiing available. The bowl is steep and requires riding a ridgeline until you pick a point to drop in. If you are looking for the ultimate experience or for first tracks, plan on doing some hiking as the easily accessed runs will get cut up pretty quick.

McConkey's is a bit smaller scale and offers skiers a great place to get double black rides without moving too far away from the rest of the mountain. You can follow the ridgeline and drop in immediately to the steeps of the bowl or continue around the bend and find a tree route through the Black Forest.

Hikers can also do some climbing and find many other in-bounds, avalanched-controlled skiing. Puma Bowl, Scotts Bowl, and Pinecone Ridge are available when the snow is good and the avalanche control is complete. However, those areas are not always open and you will need to check with the resort before venturing up there.

## Cruisers

Park City has abundant cruisers. There are tons of runs that are nicely groomed and perfect for those wanting to carve lovely turns. However, if you are looking for a guaranteed winner, you may want to check out their *Signature Runs* on the snow and grooming report.

The signature runs are those that have been given special attention by the groomers and have the best possible conditions. You can pick up a grooming report every morning in the lodge or check out the boards at the base. Either way, this is a nice way to ensure you will find a quality cruiser.

For a gentle ride, hang out on Keystone off the Thaynes Double or Mel's Alley off the Silverloade Double. If you are looking for a flat, steep drop, Crescent or Silver Skis off the Ski Team Double are the ticket. Both have an amazing pitch and great drops. You may want to check that your edges are nice and sharp.

## Bumps

For the best knee-rocking bumps in all of Park City, hit Thaynes, located just below the Thaynes lift. The run gets nicely carved bumps throughout the season and has an excellent pitch to keep your rhythm going. The Hoist is also off Thaynes and gets some equally beautiful bumps.

Off the McConkey's Six-Pack are Sunrise and Buckeye. Both are double blue runs that get groomed on occasion. If they have been left alone for a couple days, the bumps get really nice. They are especially good at the bottom, and when the run turns green, drop into the bowl for another short field.

If you want quick access to the bumps, Widowmaker and Nail Driver are directly off the Payday lift and are a lot of fun. Both offer nicely formed bumps and see a lot of traffic. In addition, the runs are crossed by an easy run called Drift, so you can escape if your legs are suffering.

## Trees and Steeps

If you are looking for the perfect glading adventure, Park City offers the Black Forest in McConkey's bowl. This deep tree forest has various access points all along Tycoon. Simply pick a route and eventually you will find yourself at the bottom of a small gulley. The bottom is a bit bumpy and not too fun if you quit early, so keep in the trees as far as possible.

The resort actually clears trees to keep it cut nicely so you can find a variety of challenging routes. However, you will want to ensure there has been enough snow before picking any path or you may be investing in a new pair of skis or snowboard.

As noted previously, for elbow-scraping steeps, check out Crescent, Silver Skis, or Shaft. These runs have awesome vertical but get groomed. This means you can generate some amazing speed and carve some really edgy turns without having to deal with the bumps.

## Powder

When the powder starts to fall, the real hounds head to Jupiter Bowl to get first tracks. There is no question that Jupiter has the best powder on the mountain and its massive size will appeal to skiers and snowboarders of expert qualifications.

However, there are many great spots on the mountain to find powder that will give you fresh tracks and you won't have to wait for avalanche control. If you want to avoid the crowds, head over to the Ski Team Double. These runs are steep and won't have people on them until the end of the day. That means less competition for fresh tracks!

Intermediate skiers will be able to get a little powder experience by taking any of the blue runs that run off the King Con Quad. An added benefit to that chair is that it crosses over each run as it ascends. An observant rider can scope out potential paths for tracks while on the lift.

## Snowboarding

Park City welcomes snowboarders! They have one of the largest half-pipes in the state, plus four varying difficulty terrain parks for riding rails and jumps. These parks vary in difficulty and provide a great way to improve those grabs, heighten your air, and most importantly, hone those landing skills.

▲ Park City's thigh-burning bumps are some of the best in Utah.

From the base you can find three of the four terrain parks and the half-pipe. Moreover, if you have got your skills accelerated move up to Jonesy's on the mountain to find some of the biggest jumps and the most challenging rails. The park is hard to find on the map. Look for it located off the Bonanza Hi-Speed Lift.

## ☺ Tips and Tricks

If you are feeling tired and the weather is right, take a trip over to the Jonesy's Terrain Park and ride to the bottom. There you will find a bench that provides a great rest spot and hours of entertainment while you watch big air and incredible blunders.

## Other Activities

Those looking for winter thrills without all the gear can take a ride on the Alpine Coaster. This winter roller coaster is for thrill seekers who are hanging out at the Resort Center. Also, only a short distance from Park City is Gorgoza Park, which offers tubing and mini snow-mobiles (yes . . . you read that right). Take the kids for as much fun as you can have off the mountain.

Park City provides immeasurable amenities for visitors. From a web site that can help you plan your runs down the mountain to extensive facilities for handicapped winter sports enthusiasts, they strive to welcome everyone to the resort.

## Lodging

Whatever you want, you can find. Whether it is a small bed and breakfast or a luxury home, Park City has plenty of lodging. You will want to book very early for holidays and certainly during the Sundance Film Festival. During other weekends, you will still want to plan ahead, but you will find a lot of options.

Park City does not own its own lodging, but it does provide a vacation planning service. In addition, there are many national chains located in the Park City area. A few easy phone calls and you should be able to find a number of excellent choices close to the resort.

## Restaurants

Food at Park City Mountain Resort is your typical skiing fare. Chili, hamburgers, and fries can be found at all the on-mountain restaurants. However, you are not relegated to eating these delicacies if you are not interested or you have a more sensitive palate.

For those wanting something more interesting, head over to the Mid-Mountain Restaurant hidden off the Pioneer Chair. It offers great full meals like a turkey dinner or lighter choices such as a fruit and cheese platter. In addition, there is a ton of seating and televisions if you need a break from all the exercise.

Gourmets who do not let fried food touch their tongue can take the Town Lift and find any number of excellent restaurants of any variety on Main Street. From wickedly hot Thai to a slice of gourmet pizza, almost every option is available. However, you may need reservations and you will want to plan the trip into town in advance.

## ☺ Tips and Tricks

A quick and effective approach to find all your restaurant options is to pick up a copy of *Park City Magazine Menu Guide*. The guide contains over 80 pages of menus and details about most the restaurants in the city. It can be found for free in most condos and hotel rooms or in magazine racks around town.

Last, the resort base does have a lot of other restaurant offerings, and while that area of the mountain does get very busy throughout the day, there are a lot of choices. You can be certain it will be packed for après ski, so you may want to plan to be early for the rush times of lunch and after your finish on the slopes.

RANAE BUNKER

# 8

# Powder Mountain Resort

## About the Resort

*Disclaimer:* The skiers and snowboarders who frequent Powder Mountain would like it to be known that the information presented in this book is being provided against their will. Also, if you visit their resort, they would like you to please keep the secret to yourself.

Imagine a place with unlimited terrain and unbelievable options. Imagine powder at every turn and every run a potential dream come true. Imagine a place where you experience the thrill of backcountry skiing on every run but find convenient transportation waiting at the bottom. This is not a fantasy. This is Powder Mountain.

Located up Ogden Canyon, Powder Mountain is the largest resort in the United States. There are 5,500 acres of terrain that only your imagination can conceive. Open fields of powder, giant cliffs, and acres and acres of glade skiing, everything you have ever dreamed of having is offered at Powder.

## ☺ Tips and Tricks

The road to Powder Mountain is very tricky. It is steep, and after a snow, a four-wheel-drive vehicle is advisable. Unlike other resorts, Powder Mountain's main center and starting point are near the top. Thus, the drive brings you up to nearly 8,000 feet to start your day on the slopes.

If you can, take the shuttle from Wolf Creek Resort. The resort is located just below Powder Mountain and it is a short bus ride to the top. They run shuttles in the morning until 10 AM. They have

P.O. Box 450
Eden, UT 84310

**Web:** www.powder
mountain.net

**E-mail:** powdermountain@
powdermountain.com

**Main:** 801-745-3772

**Snow Report:**
801-745-3771

**Ski and Snowboard
School:** 801-745-3772
(ext. 127)

**RESORT STATISTICS**

**Peak Elevation:** 8,900 feet
(2,712 meters)

**Base Elevation:** 6,895 feet
(2,101 meters)

**Vertical Drop:** 2,105 feet
(505 meters)

**Area:** 5,500 acres
(2,226 hectares)

**Night Skiing and
Snowboarding:** Yes

one at lunch and then they shuttle people down in the evening. This is perfect for people who plan to spend the whole day at the resort.

Retaining its local charm, the resort is less about frills and more about the sport. You won't find five-star accommodations or fancy restaurants. What you will find is abundant skiing and snowboarding. Powder Mountain gives you more snow for your dollar than any other resort in the state!

No matter when you visit, be prepared for a long day that will not only challenge your physical skill but your tolerance for fun. You will literally have one of the best runs of your life over and over and over again. At the end of the day, your visit to Powder Mountain will be so good you will want to keep it a secret.

## About the Mountain

Powder Mountain is astounding. First off, it is one of the largest resorts in North America yet it is serviced by five lifts. Next, the resort has incredible skiing yet only 10 percent of the entire place is actually groomed. Last, it has tons of open powder skiing, cruisers, tree skiing, and incredible steeps, but you will be hard pressed to find any real bump skiing. The place is an enigma.

Powder Mountain has to be one of the most confusing layouts of any resort in Utah. It is easy to get twisted and turned around. Part of the reason is the fact that there are two base areas and lift access goes three different directions. Yet, once you figure it all out, you will be in a state of bliss.

### ☺ Tips and Tricks

Mountain Hosts are available for complimentary tours daily at 10 AM. These tours allow you to learn the layout of the lift-accessible parts of the mountain and pretty much stick to the groomed terrain.

However, if you want to really see the entire mountain, pay a few bucks and get one of Powder's professional hosts to show it all. As your guide, he or she will take you into Powder Country, or snow-cat skiing, or over to Cobabe Canyon. You will get better information and more fun and be able to go alone into those areas.

Simply stated, Powder Mountain is massive. The landscape seems to go on forever. Looking at a trail map can't even sufficiently provide an understanding of its immense size. In fact, they print two to help those who are trying to grasp its size. The first is the main resort area with an inset and the second is for Powder Country.

▲ Powder Mountain's terrain seems to go on forever.

Powder's first area is called Sundown and is served by the Sundown Double and the Tiger Rope Tow. This area is small and hosts the night skiing. However, it is also the place to get access to the immense in-bound backcountry skiing. Thus, you may spend a lot of time in this little area but never actually ski any of it.

Powder has two areas that feel like backcountry, but both are inside the boundary of the resort and are served by lifts, shuttle buses, and a snowcat. Powder Country is accessible from both the top of the Hidden Lake Express Quad and the Sundown Double. Once you ski to the bottom, a shuttle will retrieve you and drop you back at the Sundown base or up at the main base.

The second area is serviced by a snowcat. A ticket for the cat costs a few extra bucks above a lift ticket, but it is worth every single penny. This large vehicle has been equipped to carry close to 20 people up

▲ Spectacular views surround you at Powder Mountain.

Lightening Ridge. At the top of Cobabe Peak, you are left to select any one of thousands of ways down. The bottom feeds into the Paradise Quad.

As if this was not enough, Cobabe Canyon is an entirely different area that is accessible via the Sunrise Poma lift. The area provides incredible tree skiing, and if you are prepared to hike, you'll find more untouched powder. The only real issue is that the lengthy ride out of the canyon is a bit tiring.

Powder also has the Hidden Lake, Paradise, and Timberline areas. Each provides groomed and ungroomed skiing. These are the traditional areas of the resort that most visitors explore when they come. Hidden Lake features predominantly blue and green terrain. Paradise and Timberline are the in-bound expert terrain.

▲ Endless tree skiing in deep powder can be found everywhere at Powder.

RANAE BUNKER

Overall, Powder Mountain is mostly a mountain for people passionate about the sports of skiing and snowboarding. Those new to the sport only touch on a small part of what has made this a destination for aficionados for years.

## ● Easiest Terrain

There are actually some wonderful spots for green skiers to explore at Powder Mountain. Because the resort is large, they have a number of wonderful runs where beginners can really experience the joy and excitement of skiing.

For absolute novices, you may want to begin on the Sundown Double at the lower base. The runs are much shorter and you will find your confidence growing quickly after a few quick trips. In addition, there is a great view at the top to give you the exhilaration and encouragement to explore more.

Later in the day, trek over to the Hidden Lake Express Quad. This area has a load of fun options. The runs are groomed and there are many scenic routes down to the lift. East 40 and Drifter are nice easy routes that give you a gentle start. Some of the blue skiing on this run is actually easy enough to get you started.

If you want to get really adventurous, head over to the Sunrise Poma and experience the open trees and mild slopes below Sunrise Ridge. The relaxed sloping landscape gently carries you down and expands the amount of terrain you can explore.

### ☺ Tips and Tricks

While Poma lifts are not in wide use anymore, they were very popular in the early days of skiing. The lift is very easy to use for skiers. Simply grab the bar and place the disk between your legs. However, this is much more challenging for snowboarders.

RANAE BUNKER

▲ Because of the thousands of acres of terrain, Heli skiing is also an option at Powder.

Skiers have a natural forward position when going up the Poma. However, snowboarders are turned sideways to the mountain, and as such, have to ride with their body turned sideways as the lift pulls them up the hill. This means you may need to hold the bar in an uncomfortable position while you go up.

Before jumping on, ask the lift operator to give you short instructions on how to use the Poma lift. Watch a few snowboarders take it and then give it a whirl. Chances are it will knock you down once or twice at first because the motion is very different. However, don't get frustrated. The ride to the top is short but the walk isn't. Once you get a handle on it, you will be pleased with the terrain you can access.

### ■ Intermediate Terrain

Blue skiers and snowboarders will find both the Timberline Triple and Hidden Lake Express Quad great places to spend the day. There is abundant terrain on both lifts. There are many routes to explore, and when mixed with some green, you will have a terrific day on the slopes.

The more advanced intermediates can head over to the Sundown Double for shorter but steeper blue runs. If you want even more options, take the Sunrise Poma and explore Cobabe Canyon. Most of the canyon is blue skiing. However, the end is a long drawn-out catwalk that can be exhausting at the end of the day.

Powder Country does have some intermediate routes, and if you want to step up your skills in boarding or skiing, you may want to find a friend or host to show you around. However, do not choose to explore this yourself. You may end up lost, frozen, or injured.

RANAE BUNKER

▲ Powder skiers have a hard time wiping the smile off their faces.

### ◆ Advanced Terrain

The Paradise Quad is aptly named. The expert skiing off this lift is simply incredible. Cliffs, steeps, and narrow chutes are easy to find. There are small gullies and great drops. The whole area is very challenging for any expert skier, and when the big areas are closed for avalanche control, you will want to explore these runs.

The Timberline Triple also has many excellent options for advanced and expert skiers. The steeps to the left of the chair keep you on a nice edge. You can find a lot of speed as you race to the bottom of the lift. On the right of the lift, there is a great ridgeline to ride and drop.

### ◆ ◆ Experts Only Terrain

Where do you start? The resort has literally unlimited experts only terrain. Seasoned veterans of skiing and snowboarding simply have to look at the trail map and decide where to jump off. Ideally, you

▲ Powder Mountain has two bases to accommodate its huge terrain.

will want to explore both Lightning Ridge and Powder Country.

Snowcat skiing off Lightning Ridge is an absolute must, and you will definitely want to pay the extra fee for the ride. The wait at the bottom for the snowcat is never too long and the access from Cobabe Peak is absolutely spectacular. Once on top, there are endless fields of powder waiting for you.

Powder Country is a little more foreboding as there are a lot of routes down and the unknowing visitor may get confused on where he or she is supposed to come out. Just look for the road at the bottom and hike over to the shuttle pickup. All routes back here do lead to the bottom, but you will want to be careful.

Overall, the terrain at Powder Mountain is a dream for experts. The only thing detracting from the whole experience is the time to return and do it again. The wait for the shuttle or snowcat seems like forever when you know what is waiting. The landscape is endless; the options, innumerable; and the experience, amazing.

## Cruisers

You can measure a good cruiser by either length or scenery. Either way Powder Mountain wins. For a great long run, try 3 Mile. When taken from the top of the Timberline Triple all the way down to the bottom of the Paradise Quad, it seems to go on forever.

Everything off the Sunrise Poma is great for cruising. The runs are beautiful and gentle. Groves of aspen trees decorate sloping hills that carry you softly down to the base of the Hidden Lake Express Quad. Do not miss these runs if you want a good cruise.

## Bumps

Believe it or not, there really aren't many options for bumps at Powder Mountain. Because the mountain is so large, the terrain is so spread out, and the traffic is so light, it is rare that bumps get carved properly. If you really are intent on finding bumps, there a few spots that might be an option.

On the Sundown Double you may be able to find some good bumps built directly beneath the chair. The run is called Showdown and tends to attract the night skiers. You may also get lucky if you explore the Paradise Quad. Because it is an experts only area, bumps may develop below the ridgeline in the narrow chutes.

Last, explore Whiskey Springs at the bottom of the Hidden Lake Express Quad. This run has a nice pitch and does seem to get a mogul field closer to the base of the lift.

## Trees and Steeps

Skiing in the trees at Powder Mountain is a simple exercise. The whole mountain is covered in glades of aspen and pine, and you can pick your flavor wherever you like. If you want steep, head over to Lightning Ridge. The north slope of Cobabe Canyon is an excellent place to start for intermediates.

Half of Powder Country is filled with trees and more advanced skiers will find it the perfect scene to get a deep snow fix while skiing in the woods. The glades are long with frequent openings. It is exactly how you imagine skiing in the trees in deep powder.

There is no shortage of steep terrain at Powder Mountain. However, the deep snow diminishes its impact. If it has been a while since the last snow, you will be able to find the steeps, but they may be crusted over and challenging.

▲ If you can see it, you probably can ski it at Powder Mountain.

## Powder

The name of the resort says it all. This mountain is covered in the fresh white Utah snow throughout the season and the options for making fresh tracks are unlimited. You do not have to go into Powder Country or go snowcat skiing to get to the powder. However, why wouldn't you? This is why you are visiting Powder Mountain.

The resort received the distinction of being named the number one destination for powder in North America by *Ski Magazine* in 2007. It earned the title because it has some of the best powder skiing in the nation and possibly the world. If you seek deep, white, untouched Utah snow, there is no better place to find it.

## Snowboarding

Boarders will love the long and open runs of Powder Mountain. The endless powder and great wide slopes are perfect for carving and jumping. If that isn't enough, the resort also has two terrain parks and a 400-foot-long terrain park.

Sundown Terrain Park is for all riders and is a good place to get your start if you are new to rails and tables. If you have the skills and want to be challenged, take a ride over to Hidden Lake Terrain Park.

## Lodging

Powder does have a small resort at its base called the Columbine Inn. Below the resort in the Ogden Valley, you can find Wolf Creek Resort. Both provide a wonderful place to stay if you choose to make Powder Mountain your destination resort.

If you are on a tighter budget, consider staying in Ogden. There are a lot of different options and it is only about 30 to 40 minutes to the resort from downtown. In addition, you have access to Ogden's great restaurants and nightlife for après ski.

## Restaurants

If you came to this resort looking for gourmet food, you will be sorely disappointed. Powder Mountain offers the basic ski fare with some fun options on pleasant days such as an outdoor barbecue.

The Hidden Lake Lodge provides the same basic food, but the second floor dining area has great views. On a clear day, you can see up to four states—Utah, Idaho to the north, Wyoming to the east, and Nevada to the west.

After skiing, pop into the Powder Keg for a beer and a burger. The food is fresh and tasty. The warm fireplace is a great place to end the day.

RANAE BUNKER

# 9

# Snowbasin Resort

## About the Resort

One of the wonderful parts of skiing and snowboarding is the element of discovery that you experience as you explore a mountain. Finding untracked powder, turning onto an empty run, or coming into what seems like a secret valley provides exhilaration and excitement. A visit to Snowbasin provides the same feeling but throughout the entire resort.

Back in 1939, the first skiers made their trek down the mountain and Snowbasin had its first rope tow in operation. Since that time, the resort has undergone very few changes. A few new lifts were installed, but for the most part, the mountain was a local's hangout with a small shack for lunch and ticket sales. However, this all changed in 2000.

For the first time in nearly 70 years, the resort underwent a major transformation. Being designated the home to the 2002 Winter Olympic Downhill and Super G, the entire resort was given a multimillion-dollar overhaul for the games. New lodges, new lifts, and expanded terrain were all added.

Today, the resort features world-class lodges with chandeliers, Persian carpets, and probably the nicest bathrooms you have ever seen. Two top-to-bottom gondolas transport you up the mountain in warmth and give access to boundless terrain. A high-speed quad and tram provide access to expert terrain that used to require a hike.

With these improvements, Snowbasin rivals any resort in North American. The great additions in infrastructure and lodges only built upon what is already an amazing mountain. The resort has some of

P.O. Box 460
3925 East Snowbasin Road
Huntsville, UT 84317

**Web:** www.snowbasin.com

**E-mail:** info@snowbasin.com

**Main:** 801-620-1000

**Snow Report:**
801-620-1100

**Ski and Snowboard
School:** 801-620-1016

**RESORT STATISTICS**

**Peak Elevation:** 9,350 feet
(2,849 meters)

**Base Elevation:** 6,391 feet
(1,947 meters)

**Vertical Drop:** 2,959 feet
(901 meters)

**Area:** 2,650 acres
(1072 hectares)

**Night Skiing and
Snowboarding:** No

RANAE BUNKER

▲ Snowbasin's tram carries riders to incredible views and amazing terrain.

the nicest terrain in Utah with massive fields of powder, excellent groomed runs, challenging chutes, and some of the best cruisers around.

Even with this expanded development, great effort was placed on retaining and preserving the natural beauty of the region. The towering cliffs of Mount Ogden, the dense forests of John Paul, and the wide-open space of Strawberry still feel very idyllic. It is not uncommon to see moose and other wildlife trekking through the resort.

So while the facilities and access have improved significantly since its creation, the mountain and its wonderful terrain remain unchanged. Snowbasin offers its visitors beautiful surroundings both indoors and out. It's time you discovered the secret of Snowbasin.

## About the Mountain

Snowbasin is immense. Broken into three distinctive areas, the resort offers riders open and unimpeded terrain. Middle Bowl, John Paul, and Strawberry provide limitless options for any type of skiing and snowboarding you want to explore. From gentle gliding greens to extreme expert terrain, this resort has it all.

The central area of the mountain is called Middle Bowl and it provides the largest number of options for most skiers and snowboarders. Historically, this is where the original resort has been located since the '30s and remains the most popular part of the mountain for green and blue skiers. Still, you can find anything you are looking for in Middle Bowl.

To the north of Middle Bowl is the John Paul area. Named after a World War II veteran, this part of the mountain is primarily dedicated to intermediate and expert terrain. John Paul used to be a serious hike for experts. Since the installation of a high-speed quad and the Mount Allen Tram, the terrain is easily accessible and has some of the finest skiing on the mountain.

To the south is Strawberry, and like the name, it is sweet! This area of the mountain is a powder hound's dream. The long undulating landscape makes the ride down simply perfect for experiencing

▲ Relax and enjoy the mountain top dining at Snowbasin.

Utah's powder at its finest. There are also nice groomers and some excellent cruises.

## ☺ Tips and Tricks

The top of Strawberry has a beautiful view of the Ogden area and provides the opportunity to stand on top of a mountain. There are great spots for photographs. Everyone who is an intermediate or better skier should take at least one gondola ride to the top for the experience.

However, keep in mind that being on top of a mountain does present challenges. On a bad weather day, the view will be gone and you may want to avoid the gondola entirely. Strawberry has a tendency to get fogged in. In fact, it is cloud cover that makes getting down from the top challenging for even experienced skiers and snowboarders.

The convenience and comfort of the Snowbasin gondolas will spoil you for any other resort. A single ride up will convince you that chairlifts are barbaric. Sitting in the warmth of the cabin as you ascend

▲ Exciting events and activities continue throughout the season at Utah resorts.

quickly to the top, you will not want to ski anywhere else but on the Strawberry and Middle Bowl area of the resort.

In addition to their incredible comfort, the gondolas also service thousands of skiers per hour. That means that even on the busiest day of the year, the lift lines are almost non-existent. You may stand for a few minutes as eight people at a time get into the cars for the ride to the top.

While the chairs are nowhere as nice as the gondolas, they do access some of the best terrain on the mountain. While exploring the resort, you may want to break down and take a few chairs so you can explore the terrain that can't be as easily accessed from the gondolas.

Many people miss some of the skiing from the top of the Porcupine Triple because they ski exclusively from the gondola. However, there are far more (and often interesting) options if you deviate from the normal paths created by all the other skiers and snowboarders and explore the entire mountain.

The layout of Snowbasin in the Middle Bowl area has two congestion spots. On very busy day, Bear Hollow and the lower part of Needles Run below the Porcupine lift will have a lot of people heading to the bottom. People seem to congregate and often stop as they decide what route to take to the base.

A quick glance at the trail map will show you there are a lot of alternate routes. Check out where you are and then select a route that avoids these trouble spots. For example, a quick cut over onto Stewart's will take you to Wildcat Bowl and give you a straight shot to the bottom.

In all, Snowbasin needs to be explored. The resort is not simply about the two gondolas but about the vast amount of skiing and snowboarding available. A few *uncomfortable* lift rides will reveal a lot of great terrain and allow you to enjoy everything this mountain has to offer.

▼ Author takes a few turns at his home resort

### ● Easiest Terrain

While it may be tempting to jump on the gondola for a ride to the top, there is no green route from the top. The Little Cat Double will provide a few beginner runs to warm up and then a ride up the Becker Triple will place you on some nice gentle greens for starters.

If you are eager to see the top of the Needles Express Gondola, you don't have to ski or snowboard to the bottom. There is downhill service so you can enjoy lunch at the top. Green skiers will need some time to get comfortable with the terrain, altitude, and equipment before taking on the entire mountain.

### ■ Intermediate Terrain

Riding from the top of the Needles Express Gondola provides so many choices that you may be a bit overwhelmed. Just below the

▲ The Snowbasin terrain is diverse and challenging for all levels of skiers and snowboarders.

RANAE BUNKER

summit are a lot of wonderful intermediate trails of varying degrees of difficulty. All of them are well groomed and very wide.

The intermediate runs over on the Strawberry Gondola are slightly more advanced. The terrain is a bit steeper, but it is also a lot wider, providing ample room for everyone to stop and take a breath. Blue skiers should have good control of their speed and turning before venturing over to this side of the mountain.

### ☺ Tips and Tricks

The John Paul Express Quad is for experts only, almost. There is one run off the chair that is blue and it is a great one. Mount Ogden Bowl is a long run that winds its way through the base of the bowl. It hugs the side of the hill for a bit and has some great turns.

There is a lot of blue at Snowbasin. Intermediates will find many wide-open, easy-to-turn runs for their enjoyment. There are some steep areas for blue skiing, but the runs are normally groomed and there are a number of traverses for people whose ability isn't up to the terrain.

## ◆ Advanced Terrain

Black diamond skiing and snowboarding is available throughout the mountain. However, the John Paul Express Quad is exclusively dedicated to this type of terrain. Riders looking for steeps, bumps, cliffs, and other challenging mountain features will find some great choices off this lift.

Off the Strawberry Express Gondola, you will find most of the expert terrain is located to skier's right over in the bowls. The groomed terrain is predominantly blue and is over to the left. The split between the expert and intermediate terrain occurs rather quickly and does not converge again until the bottom.

Snowbasin has numerous ridgelines to ride, and from those you can find some wonderful expert terrain to explore. Philpot, John Paul, Hollywood, and Wildcat all ride the top of ridges and have steep and sometimes bumpy terrain below.

## ☺ Tips and Tricks

The ridgelines at Snowbasin often separate base access. Depending on the side you choose, you may end up on a different lift or gondola from where you started. For example, taking Philpot to skier's left will bring you to the base and to the right will bring you to Strawberry. Be certain to coordinate with your friends or family to define which side you plan to ride or you may end up a mountain apart.

Another distinctive feature of the expert terrain is the steep and fast runs over in the John Paul area. Home to the 2002 Winter Olympics, the runs the racers competed on are still in place and still provide fierce speeds. If you want the thrill and exhilaration of what a racer feels, give the Grizzly or Wildflower runs a try.

## ◆ ◆ Experts Only Terrain

Snowbasin features abundant natural terrain for the double black diamond skier. There are routes from literally anywhere on the mountain to explore extreme drops, cliffs, and chutes. Many of the more challenging and unique will require some climbing or hiking. However, there is a lot directly off the gondolas and lifts.

One good way to start is to ride to the top of the Mount Allen Tram and then traverse the mountaintop to find a good place to drop in. The view from the top is great and your ego will be pumped when the tram operator explains to the passengers that the terrain you are accessing is experts only.

Most of the terrain accessible off the John Paul Express Quad on skier's left is experts only. However, the tram will give you that extra vertical you need to get to the really challenging stuff. A ride up the Porcupine Triple will give you access to some of the landscape viewable from John Paul above Mount Ogden Bowl.

Over on Strawberry, you can exit to right when you get off the gondola and ride high over to some great terrain. It is not immediately apparent when you get off on the top that the route is accessible. However, if you keep your vertical you will have no issue getting over to some of the terrain off DeMoisy Peak.

In the opposite direction you will find Sister's Bowl. Avalanche control is a serious concern as the mountain face is very steep. However, if the gates are open, this is some of the most beautiful skiing in the world. The bowl rides right up against the mountain and you can't believe the thrill of having these massive peaks shadowing you while you descend.

## Cruisers

Cruising is an art form at Snowbasin. The wide and open terrain make it perfectly suited to cruise, turn, and cruise some more. In reality, there are so many great options that it is hard to narrow it down. Most of the runs from the top of the Needles Express Gondola will give you great cruising. Just pick a route down and you will find a wide-open route for making turns.

One top-to-bottom route that will test your legs but is worth every turn starts on the Porcupine Traverse. Take the traverse across and follow the natural flow into Needles Run. Pass the Porcupine Triple and follow it to skier's right to take it down to the base via Blue Grouse.

Main Street in the Strawberry area is very wide, beautifully groomed, and super long. It is perfect for snowboarders looking for long wide turns. The bottom turns into a very wide canyon. The sides almost feel like a wide half-pipe. The last portion of the ride, just before the gondola, flattens out and you will need to maintain your speed.

One of the best places to cruise in the resort is Dan's Run. From the top of the Strawberry Traverse, Dan's takes you on a wonderful rollercoaster ride with steep drops smoothing into level gentle cruises. The only issue is that when there hasn't been grooming for a couple

◄ Ski technology has greatly improved the fun and ease of the sport resorts.

of days, the steep portions do develop bumps. However, after fresh snow you can fly.

## Bumps

Snowbasin has a lot of options for bumps, but strangely, you will probably find more blue terrain bumped up than many of the black runs. The reason for this is the layout of the mountain. Moguls are formed by many skiers and snowboarders consistently carving turns on a particular run. Snowbasin's layout funnels skiers and boarders to the bottom creating mogul fields on the common routes.

Intermediate skiers will find moguls on City Hall, the Becker Face, the steeps on Dan's, and over on the side of Herbert's. The bumps are usually a very manageable size and are good for working on your skills. If these runs get a good grooming, they may smooth up, but it doesn't take long for the bumps to return.

Experts will find good bumps as well. Pork Barrel directly off the top of the Needles Express Gondola is always nicely carved. Any of the runs directly over the Hollywood ridgeline get some great bumps. You can check them out when you ride over on the John Paul Express Quad.

▲ Snowbasin is known for its wide-open runs and expansive terrain.

Strawberry doesn't get as many because its expansive terrain isn't suited to bump development. However, Carnahan's does develop a decent-sized field, and on occasion, the top of The Diamond will get nice bumps. However, your best bet will be in the main mountain area where traffic is heavier.

Back in the old days, 25th Street of the Becker Triple, Becks just above Porcupine Triple base, and Pineview above the Middle Bowl base would get some of the best on the mountain. Yet, the gondola has reduced the traffic to those runs. You may want to check them out though if there hasn't been a dump for a while. Some of the old guys who ski *The Basin* can't break their habits.

## Trees and Steeps

Glade skiing and snowboarding at Snowbasin is really great. Conversely, the runs are sometimes a challenge to find and require

▲ Hitting chutes at Snowbasin requires some climbing but the payback is dramatic.

a careful eye. Many of the best tree areas are also home to large cliffs, big holes, and sudden drops that will knock the wind out of you. Experts only should venture into the trees.

From the top of the John Paul Express Gondola, ride over to Apron. Just below the bowl the trees start to get dense. Cross the run named Mount Ogden Bowl and keep descending. The terrain continues to be steep and dumps out onto Needles Run. The whole trek downward is tree covered and fun.

Bear Wallow is a touch hard to find and takes a lot of ridge riding to get to but has some nice glades for exploring. It's easier if you take the Becker Triple and then stay high along Slo Road over to Dwayne's. The area between Dwayne's and Bear Wallow can have some brush if the snow isn't deep enough. Otherwise it's a blast.

The face of the Grizzly Downhill will make you wonder if snow can physically stay on a face this steep. Take the tram to the top to take on this vertical drop. Then on your way down, pop off the John

▲ Snowbasin has two mountain-top lodges with spectacular food and views.

RANAE BUNKER

Paul ridge to discover even more steeps. This whole side of the mountain has a lot of steep terrain to experience.

## Powder

Powder can be found all over Snowbasin after a good dump. Its wide-open terrain and great mountain layout give everyone a chance to have a blast in the fresh snow. However, there is a place that the powder is simply magical and that is Strawberry. From top to bottom it is one of the best powder runs Utah has to offer.

A ride through Strawberry is like having a blank canvas to paint. The wide-open fields of powder are almost empty of trees or rocks. The area is almost featureless except for the rising and falling landscape. All you have is the blue sky and white snow to carry you down to the bottom.

To some, the experience of powder skiing or snowboarding Strawberry is almost overwhelming. Visitors howl and scream as they descend. A ride down White Lightning or through Moonshine Bowl can feel like an epiphany. If you are very lucky, avalanche control on Sisters Bowl will be complete.

The almost insane concept here is that this is only one part of the whole powder package at Snowbasin. The other side of the mountain is just as wonderful, albeit a bit more covered with trees and obstacles and a touch harder to access. A drop into Easter Bowl or Wheeler does require a ride up the tram and a short hike.

Intermediate skiers wanting a taste of powder should ride the Becker Triple to the top and experience Willow Springs. Its long gentle pitch is the perfect training ground for powder novices. In addition, the run out to the bottom is not too long and you can practice over and over again.

## Snowboarding

Snowboarders will find a lot of fun snowboarding features besides the great wide-open slopes. The resort supports three different terrain parks spread around the mountain. One is over in Coyote Bowl, another is on the Porky Face, and the most popular is located right at the base.

Snowbasin has both natural and man-made half-pipes. Its four natural half-pipes are located in varying spots on the mountain, but all of it is expert terrain. The resort also has a giant super pipe measuring in at 340 feet long by 17 feet high. The pipe has its own tow rope and is located over at the base of the women's finish for the Olympics.

## Other Activities

If you think alpine skiing is beautiful here, Snowbasin has a wonderful 26km trail system for cross-country skiing just below the base of the resort. Even better, they provide this whole area free of charge. Best of all, there are additional areas surrounding the resort offered by the forest service.

If you want to break away and play, the resort also has a wonderful tubing park for kids and adults alike. Built on the remains of the Olympic Downhill finish, it is a great activity for people tired of skiing or snowboarding. Six lanes of tubing are serviced by a handle tow lift so you don't need to walk back up after your ride.

# Lodging

While there is no lodging directly at the resort, the Ogden Valley and Ogden area have many wonderful choices and are about the same distance from the resort. Both provide easy access to Snowbasin and highlight their close proximity to the resort as a benefit of staying in the area.

# Restaurants

Snowbasin believes that dining is part of the entire vacation experience and offers some of the best food around. Dining in each of the three lodges not only provides wonderful gourmet food but offers ski fare that is a step above the norm. In addition, they feature local beers and full dinners, and they do a Sunday brunch.

# 10

# Snowbird Resort

## About the Resort

Many people trek across the globe to experience the sophistication and style of resorts in Austria, Italy, or France. Yet, nestled up Little Cottonwood Canyon, you can get a taste of what those resorts are like. Elegant and modern conveniences combined with Old World charm, Snowbird evokes the atmosphere and charisma of European resorts while maintaining the hospitality of the American West.

When you arrive at Snowbird, you will immediately notice it is different than any other ski resort you may have visited. The lodges are architecturally distinct, a tram ascends from the village to the summit, and the scenery is rustic and rugged. The whole atmosphere feels as if you have been transported to an extraordinary location. In fact, you have.

Snowbird follows other resorts by featuring a full-service spa, shopping, and more than 20 restaurants for visitors to enjoy. However, they go above others by furnishing their guests rooftop pools, ice skating, tubing, and a variety of camps for kids and adults. They make taking a real vacation easy by providing both the expected and unexpected.

For this reason, Snowbird has been known as a top resort in the United States for more than 30 years. Its incredible beauty combined with its vast array of amenities makes it a key destination for visitors from around the world. Some come for the amazing accommodations, others for the incredible food. However, most come for the snow.

Snowbird rivals Alta for the best snow in Utah. Because they share a similar altitude and location, both resorts get the lightest,

Highway 210
Little Cottonwood Canyon
Snowbird, UT 84092

**Web:** www.snowbird.com

**E-mail:** info@snowbird.com

**Main:** 801-933-2222

**Snow Report:**
801-933-2100

**Ski and Snowboard
School:** 801-933-2170

**RESORT STATISTICS**

**Peak Elevation:** 11,000 feet
(3,353 meters)

**Base Elevation:** 7,600 feet
(2,316 meters)

**Vertical Drop:** 3,240 feet
(988 meters)

**Area:** 2,500 acres
(1,012 hectares)

**Night Skiing and
Snowboarding:** Yes

▲ Snowbird has some of the most epic and sweeping views of Utah's resorts.

driest, and most abundant powder in the state. The amazing landscape at Snowbird also provides a huge number of opportunities to enjoy Utah's great snow.

Snowbird is a complete resort with everything you might want in a single location. Unlike other areas, the whole place is a single cohesive package designed to give you the best of everything. Why trek across the globe for European elegance when you get it right here in the heart of the Wasatch Front.

## About the Mountain

Many people associate words like challenging, aggressive, or hardcore with Snowbird. There is a large perception that this mountain is exclusively for skilled boarders and skiers. However, nothing could be further from the truth. Snowbird strives to provide all types of terrain for all types of riders.

Certainly, many of Utah's tightest steeps, biggest bumps, and fiercest terrain can be found at *The Bird*. Yet, Snowbird also has wonderful cruisers, excellent learning facilities, and a very manageable mountain. Focused on attracting families, this resort has opened up a lot of blue and green skiing on its lower terrain.

## ☺ Tips and Tricks

Tram or no tram? Snowbird is the only resort in Utah with a real tram. Carrying as many as 125 people to the top of the mountain in a mere eight minutes, it is a Snowbird trademark. Yet, while the ride is exhilarating and the views are spectacular, is it worth the extra cost? The short answer is *not really*.

With the Peruvian High-Speed Quad and a tunnel to Mineral Basin, the tram has become a bit redundant. Snowbird has now provided another easy way to get anywhere you want on the mountain. The tram remains the only way to get to the top in one ride and it will get you to the backside faster.

People who want to hit the peak first, need a fast ride to the top, or simply want to experience riding in the tram should not hesitate to buy a ticket. On the other hand, the mountain is completely accessible without a tram ticket, and if you want to save a few bucks, you may want to pass.

Snowbird boasts some of the best snowfall in Utah. In fact, they keep their resort open longer than the others. Their high altitude combined with their continuous visitors throughout the year make Snowbird a great early and late season option. You can often hit the slopes in early November and into May.

Runs at Snowbird are long. A quick glance at a trail map and it will appear that there are fewer runs. However, with the largest vertical drop of any resort in the state, the runs are simply a lot longer. Runs like Chip's, Silver Fox, and Primrose Path all can be skied from summit to base.

▼ You will find Snowbird tries to accommodate the whole family.

SNOWBIRD RESORT

▲ Snowbird has a lot of steep and a lot of deep.

The resort has three distinct areas. Beneath Hidden Peak is predominantly expert skiing with a few intermediate runs interspersed. The area is called Peruvian Gulch and it is celebrated for its extreme terrain. Peruvian features large towering valley walls and a great wide run at the base of the valley.

Mineral Basin resides on the backside of the mountain and holds Snowbird's best powder skiing. The terrain is mostly comprised of a large open bowl that is sparsely decorated with trees. However, underneath and around the Baldy Express Quad, there are some nice trees and gentle terrain.

Last, the Gad Valley is the area for everyone. The experts love to hang out on the Little Cloud Double for its amazing steeps and bumps. They also trek over to Thunder Bowl to explore some steep glade skiing. Intermediates have a few great runs up top, and all levels are served from the bottom of the resort.

## ● Easiest Terrain

Snowbird does not have a lot of easier terrain. However, it does not mean they don't care about beginners. Quite the contrary, they strive to provide enough terrain, but the layout of the mountain offers up a number of challenges. If you take your time, you will find some great snow to explore.

If you are completely new to skiing and snowboarding, the Chickadee lift is where you want to start. This wide and gentle slope not only services the Cliff Lodge and its guests, it is where the ski school and beginners congregate. Watch for the *Snowbird* and friends. He does make an appearance here for the kids.

The most common area that all green skiers head to at Snowbird is the Mid-Gad Double. From there, an extra wide and comfortable run called Big Emma lets you ski all day. Most people will hang out here while they get their comfort level up to explore other blue runs.

## ☺ Tips and Tricks

There is a Midway Unloading Station on the Mid-Gad Double. You do not have to ride all the way up. This convenience is for people who are just getting familiar with their equipment and want a short ride. It is also a faster way to get back to the base!

## ■ Intermediate Terrain

Intermediate skiers will find they have a few very nice options at Snowbird. The resort has positioned a number of runs off the Gad 2 Double that provide some fun canyon treks. It is especially nice to ride Bassackwards from top to bottom and get a long and refreshing ride.

Similarly, the lengthy Chip's Run is another top-to-bottom experience. Take the Peruvian Express Quad from the base. If you want, slip into the tunnel and go over into Mineral Basin to find some great blue skiing in the back. The runs may be a bit more challenging, but the wide-open terrain should give you some confidence.

## ☺ Tips and Tricks

Snowbird wanted to give more intermediate skiers access to Mineral Basin and made a single improvement that is almost too astounding to believe. They tunneled directly through the mountain and now

▲ Riding the rails at The Bird.

intermediate skiers can make an easy trek over to incredible terrain that was previously inaccessible.

The 595-foot conveyor system actually transports you through the mountain. On the opposite side you will find a nice green run you can take to the bottom and then hang out on the intermediate and beginning slopes. Once you are finished, Chip's will bring you back to the base.

### ◆ Advanced Terrain

There isn't a better resort in Utah for the expert skier. Snowbird's diverse and often notoriously tough terrain is not for the faint of heart. There is collection of advanced slopes of all types. Narrow chutes, jagged cliffs, hair-raising steeps, monster bumps, and unyielding length make Snowbird one resort to conquer.

Much of what makes Snowbird appealing to the expert skier is its variety of options. The mountain features a veritable endless menu of choices, which are all easily accessible from a variety of spots on the mountain. While some resorts note the fact that they have blue or green runs available off every lift, Snowbird offers expert terrain off every lift but one.

## ◆ ◆ Experts Only Terrain

Welcome to the dark side. Snowbird is home to the *blackest of black* terrain in Utah. Cliffs, chutes, and bumps that scare even the hardest nosed pros can be found at The Bird. Prepare yourself for brutally steep terrain, never-ending moguls, and some of Utah's most nerve-shaking landscape.

More than a third of the resort is committed to the expert rider and you should take advantage of it. Part of the allure of Snowbird is the rugged beauty that provides the atmosphere for experts to savor their extreme moments. The mountain does not simply have difficult runs but it looks nasty.

## ☺ Tips and Tricks

One of the best ways to keep you occupied on the double blacks is to take the Cirque Traverse and ride across and select a place to drop in on either side. Every run below will give you a wondrous thrill and a serious challenge. Simply cruise along until something looks appealing and then prepare for one heck of a ride.

The towering gray cliffs and jagged peaks are the perfect setting for you to experience the challenges of Snowbird. It not only helps you enjoy the experience, it makes you respect and appreciate the beauty of your surroundings. You will certainly find a lot of great spots to inspire stories that you can share with your friends.

## Cruisers

Where Snowbird doesn't have quantity in cruisers, it makes up in quality. Many of the best cruises on the mountain use almost the entire 3,240 feet (988 meters) of vertical. Not many resorts offer this amount of vertical and length and the opportunity to ride it all from top to bottom.

You can't ask for a better cruiser than Chip's Run. This lengthy and fast cruiser is a run that winds its way on the Peruvian side of the mountain. The best thing about Chip's is that it will be groomed and it will be smooth. Take the Peruvian Express Quad and start flying.

▲ Snowbird's high elevation allows abundant snowfall and Utah's longest ski season.

Regulator Johnson is a steeper expert run but a great cruiser nonetheless. It is really fun to start fast on Regulator and then finish it out on Bassackwards (Lower and Lowest). Starting from the top of the Little Cloud Double, move from Regulator over to Bassackwards. This winds its way down to the lift base of the Gadzoom High-Speed Quad.

## Bumps

Moguls from the gentle to the giant can be found throughout the resort. Depending on your flavor, you can select a number of different routes down. The best for experts is located in Little Cloud Bowl where either side of the lift gets carved continuously. Choose Shireen or Regulator Johnson to find fields to your liking.

For more relaxed bumps, try Mark Malu Fork off the Road to Provo. In addition, off to the side of Chip's in many areas, you can find trailing mogul fields that offer smaller options but still have a nice rhythm. In fact, if you ski any blue piste at Snowbird, keep your eyes on the neighboring runs. There may be some good bump challenges bordering it.

## Trees and Steeps

Steeps are really steep at Snowbird. Over on the Bookends in Mineral Basin, you can find some great drops with a view of the valley floor. Most of the terrain of Peruvian Basin has great steeps. Regulator Johnson off Little Cloud is also a great drop. However, ridges are the place to find the best drops. Simply follow the traverses and you can define your pitch by simply looking down.

Dropping off the High Baldy Traverse, there are many that seem to defy gravity. You can also ride over to Thunder Bowl off the Gad 2 Quad. If the snow is deep, it's a great descent. Finally, as already noted, the Cirque Traverse has the most options for steeps. They become especially vertical under the tram. Great Scott on the upper part and Mach Schnell on the lower will show those tram riders you got the stuff . . . or not.

▲ The runs are long and fun at Snowbird.

## Powder

There isn't a spot at Snowbird without wonderful powder. The whole mountain gets incredible snow, and you simply have to pick a spot to find good powder. The only decision you need to make is how deep you want it and how fast you want to go down.

For a nice balance of both speed and pitch, the best place is in Mineral Basin. Like a big bowl, the snow gathers there and provides boundless choices for people looking to cut fresh tracks. Simply ride the upper traverse, appropriately named The Path to Paradise, and choose your heavenly route down.

▲ The whole family will find something to like at Snowbird.

Intermediate skiers can even give the deep snow a try on Junior's Powder Paradise. This run is a great place to introduce you to Utah's legendary snow. Intermediates will ride to the outside where the pitch is not too aggressive but the snow is just as good.

## ☺ Tips and Tricks

If the weather forecaster is predicting an overnight storm, Snowbird has a program for you. First Tracks gives you almost an hour of guided morning skiing or snowboarding in the fresh snow. You will ride to the top in the tram and then your guide will show you the way. This program is for advanced intermediates and experts only.

If open whitewashed powder is not your thing, continue to the far side of the basin and the Bookends. You will find trees and some amazing steeps as you ride the outside ridgeline. The drop is nearly straight down but the deep powder will slow you down.

## Snowboarding

Picking a place to play is probably the biggest problem for snowboarders at Snowbird. Two terrain parks and a super pipe are easy to access. The super pipe and intermediate park require a ride on the Mid-Gad Double directly off the Midway exit. Thus, there is no need to ride all the way to the top and you can make quicker loops. The more advanced terrain park is located off the Baby Thunder lift.

Boarders will also love Mineral Basin. Its wide-open bowl is the perfect platform for snowboarding. Its wide-open terrain is a great place to carve massive turns and fly at top speed. Try Junior's Powder Paradise for a great fast ride with lots of lips and jumps for good natural air.

## Lodging

Towering above the base of Snowbird, the Cliff Lodge stands as much an icon of the resort as the mountain tram. People recognize and know the Cliff as a place of quality, style, and European elegance. While this may be the cornerstone of Snowbird's lodging, it is only a template for their other facilities.

No matter where you stay at Snowbird, you can expect the best in service and accommodations. From large flat screens in your room to a world-class day spa, everything has been considered. The resort succeeds in giving its visitors the quintessential European-style experience.

## Restaurants

Snowbird has a reputation for many things. Its incredible skiing and stunning scenery may be the most well known part of this reputation. However, they are also known for their excellent food. Whether you are simply stopping for a break from skiing or looking for some fine dining, Snowbird has some wonderful options.

### ☺ Tips and Tricks

A trip to Snowbird needs to include dinner at The Steak Pit. Every night, they have a visit from two or three of the biggest porcupines

▲ The world famous Cliff Lodge is distinctive for its architecture and wonderful service.

SNOWBIRD RESORT

you have ever seen. Larry and his fellow spiny friends come and dine like royalty on the restaurant's fresh bread. And by the way, the porcupines are not the only ones who find the food first-class at The Steak Pit.

On the mountain, Mid-Gad is an exceptionally popular spot to stop for a bite. The food is good and it is a convenient location for a break from all the fun. However, it is not hard to get to fine dining at the Resort Center. Simply ride back to the base and go into the center. Inside the choices abound.

## ☺ Tips and Tricks

If you are in a hurry to get back onto the mountain, General Gritts Deli in the Snowbird Center on Level 1 has inexpensive yet excellent sandwich choices. It is simply the best way to get good food at cheap prices at the resort.

# 11

# Solitude Mountain Resort

## About the Resort

In some cases, a name says it all. While many of Utah's resorts have been building up their infrastructure to accommodate more and more visitors, Solitude has been investing in keeping their resort simple, peaceful, and beautiful. A visit here is an opportunity to reconnect with nature, friends, and family.

The resort has been around for many years but has gone through a rebirth over the last 10 years. Rather than putting in fast new lifts, they have built a resort focused on helping people slow down. The construction of a European-style village, the addition of restaurants, and the improvements at the Moonbeam Base are excellent comforts for their guests.

Solitude is all about being relaxed and comfortable. They want you to come here and ski at your own pace and not feel rushed. Unlike other resorts, if you come up and the weather turns bad, you can ski on the same ticket tomorrow. If you want to slip a run or two in after work, it's not a problem. You see, Solitude doesn't sell lift tickets, they sell fulfillment.

Solitude uses a unique electronic ticketing system. Of course, you can purchase a day pass (which does not carry over to the next day) as you can at other resorts. However, you can also buy ride tickets. At every lift, there is a turnstile. Every time you take a lift, it deducts one from the card. If you only take eight, you can come back the next day and use the other two.

In addition, if you buy 10 and decide to ski more, there is no extra cost. Solitude only deducts a maximum of 10 rides a day. Thus, a

12000 Big Cottonwood
  Canyon
Solitude, UT 84121

**Web:** www.skisolitude.com

**E-mail:** info@skisolitude.com

**Main:** 801-534-1400

**Snow Report:**
  801-536-5777

**Ski and Snowboard
  School:** 801-536-5730

**RESORT STATISTICS**

**Peak Elevation:** 10,035 feet
  (3,058 meters)

**Base Elevation:** 7,988 feet
  (2,435 meters)

**Vertical Drop:** 2,047 feet
  (623 meters)

**Area:** 1,200 acres
  (486 hectares)

**Night Skiing and
  Snowboarding:** No

▲ Solitude provides a mixture of Old World and Western charm.

person could buy a 20-ride ticket and spread it over three days. This kind of flexibility and thoughtfulness is at the heart of Solitude's goal to help you enjoy your visit to their resort.

And enjoy this resort, you will. Solitude is a beautiful and peaceful spot among the Utah resorts. Nothing is hurried or contrived. Its natural scenery and slopes are stunning. They bring together a variety of accommodations and dining options to give each visitor a complete and wonderful experience.

## About the Mountain

The front side of the mountain is the most widely skied and accessed portion. All the lifts on this mountain, except for one, service this area. The strange thing is most of the people who visit Solitude will never go into what is widely regarded as their jewel. This is Honeycomb Canyon.

Honeycomb Canyon is a double black area that gets some of Utah's best powder. It is wide, long, and deep. The canyon has a ton of great skiing and yet it is not exactly easy to access. The challenge of Honeycomb Canyon is simply a matter of where to put a lift.

Solitude has opted to retain the natural beauty of the canyon, and as such, there are no lifts directly from the base to the top. If you want to fully experience this amazing place, you will have to take at least two different lifts. There is no easy way to the top of the canyon. At best, you can enter in the middle.

Regardless, the vast majority of people who visit this resort are not going to care about access to Honeycomb. They will find the service and options on the front of the mountain to be perfect.

The Eagle Express area is a delight for visitors. An entire section of the resort is dedicated exclusively to groomed, intermediate runs. For people wanting to get the most out of their day, this is the place to hang out. The lift is fast and the terrain has a lot of variety but all the same level.

## ● Easiest Terrain

Solitude has a lot of terrain for the new skier and the beginner. Unlike many resorts, they have a significant number of easy runs and all of them are well maintained. Effectively, the whole base area is dedicated to providing comfort to those who are new to skis and snowboards.

If you have never skied or snowboarded before, the Link Double is the place to work on your ability. The area does get a touch busy in the afternoon, so work on that form in the morning and move up to Moonbeam later in the day.

The Moonbeam Triple offers a lot of options. Many of the runs are very gentle and wide and provide a good starting place for beginners. If you are feeling adventurous, the Sunrise Quad also provides access to more green runs. There are also a few gentle intermediate runs in the same neighborhood to help you step up to the next level.

## ■ Intermediate Terrain

The Eagle Express Quad is a virtual paradise for intermediate skiers. Off this high-speed lift, there are so many choices you may not know where to begin. Some are on the smooth groomed side, while others add a bit of challenge to the equation. In the end, you can spend the entire day on this lift and still not explore all of its terrain.

▲ Honeycomb Canyon provides unparalleled powder skiing.

## ☺ Tips and Tricks

If you are not staying at the resort and are driving in to ski Solitude, park at the Moonbeam Base. The lot at the main lodge is much smaller and fills fast. Also, you can ski down to the Eagle Express and get a fast start on the day.

The Apex Double is another option for blue skiers. The lift is shorter and will allow you to get a few runs. It is close to the base so it might be a good choice in the morning for warm-up runs or late in the day when you are trying to slip in a few before the mountain closes.

The Sunrise Triple to the Summit Double is a bit on the hard side for intermediate skiers. It is a blue area but the runs are steeper, and if you are just starting at this level, you may want to avoid the area. If you are working on moving up to the black diamond skiing, this is the place to explore.

▲ Deep powder is found across Solitude.

## ☺ Tips and Tricks

If you want to experience the beauty of Honeycomb Canyon but are not prepared to ski it, Woodlawn is an option. This lengthy run at the bottom of the canyon is an advanced intermediate run that provides breathtaking views. It runs out to the Honeycomb Return Quad.

## ◆ Advanced Terrain

On the main part of the mountain, the only easily accessible expert terrain is on the Powder Horn Double. This terrain is actually quite nice and finishes out on some intermediate terrain. However, there is some fun to be had. The bumps grow in this area and the terrain is demanding.

Ride Eagle Ridge and drop into anything that looks good. All of it is great. If you want to move to some tougher terrain, you can slip

▲ Solitude is more than just a name. It is a philosophy at this resort.

over into the Black Forest. This is steep and deep with trees. Only experts should even considering venturing forward. However, if you can handle it, the terrain is excellent.

If you are venturing into black diamond skiing for the first time, ski or snowboard off the Summit Double. This chair services one large black area called the Headwall Forest. As you ride up you can take a peak at what you are about to tackle. If you are not up to it, the blues up here offer a fun and challenging alternative.

## ◆ ◆ Experts Only Terrain

Solitude boasts many options for the expert skier. However, of those options, the prize is really Honeycomb Canyon. Its towering cliffs and steep walls provide an exciting place to explore. The canyon has a distinct bowl shape, and depending on where you enter, you have a lot of different types of skiing and snowboarding.

▲ Options abound in
Honeycomb Canyon.

## ☺ Tips and Tricks

You do *not* want to take the 3.2-mile (5.15km) run called Woodlawn. It is slow and flat and will consume your day. Grab the Honeycomb Return Quad. It will drop you right back into the heart of the resort.

Also, do not lose your speed on Woodlawn or you will be pushing yourself back to the chair. The run is very flat and—snowboarders beware—it is also very long.

Entering from the Summit Chair, you have two options. You can either ride the traverse across and find a route down that looks good to you, or you can simply drop into the canyon and find a mixed route down. The canyon ride is not very challenging, but it does offer a great view. The farther you ride on the traverse, the more you have to hike.

If you enter Honeycomb Canyon from the top of the Powder Horn Double, you can drop immediately into the Black Forest. This

▲ Stunning scenery and abundant snowfall are all part of the Solitude experience.

side is significantly different from the opposite side of the canyon. While the traverse side is open and bowl-like, the forest side is thick with trees and has a few narrow paths down.

Also off Powder Horn is a series of super steep, double black runs. Middle Slope, Parachute, and Milk Run are fierce but fun. If you are looking for some steep pitches, this may be the best place at Solitude to find them.

## Cruisers

The Eagle Express Quad is the valley of the cruisers. All the runs provide great groomed terrain at a comfortable yet effective pitch. You will find yourself carving beautiful turns on corduroy slopes if you get to the mountain early enough.

If you really want to get some speed, take a ride over to the Summit Double chair and give Dynamite a try. This run is excellent.

It winds down the canyon like a race course driving you to the bottom of the lift. It is fast and fun.

For the more advanced skier, the pitch on Challenger off the Eagle Express Quad is worthy of those wanting a fast and steep drop. It is nothing short. It is the only black run in this area, and as such, sees very little traffic.

## Bumps

Bumps seem to keep their place at Solitude. Concord and Paradise off the Powder Horn Double will give any bump skier some excitement. They are both long and have nicely carved moguls. They are especially good after some fresh snow.

Some of the other areas of the mountain do get bumped up but it changes with the snowfall. It is best to check the grooming report before determining where to seek out the moguls. You may find that they have been smoothed out.

## Trees and Steeps

There are a lot of great spots to find tree runs at Solitude. Off the Summit Double, the Headwall is a deep and steep forest with narrow runs and loads of trees. It is a blast, and riding up the chair provides a great perspective on how steep the runs actually are.

Over in Honeycomb Canyon, the Black Forest and Navarone are both excellent areas with a lot of variables. You can choose a number of ways down and find an exciting and different route on each trip.

For the steeps, hop off the top of the Powder Horn Double and ski down any of those double black diamond runs. Milk Run is especially steep and you may even find some cliffs hidden among these very tight chutes.

## Powder

There is no question that Honeycomb Canyon is the best spot on the mountain for untouched powder. Its massive traverse allows unlimited options for dropping in to the deep snow whenever you feel the need or just get tired of hiking. It is an open bowl with powder shots galore.

If your goal is to get uncut powder, you need to continue on the traverse as long as possible. The farther you go, the more likely you will find uncut snow. However, any point you choose to drop into Honeycomb is going to be fantastic. It is powder heaven.

Intermediate skiers wanting to learn the ways of powder skiing are encouraged to hang out on the runs on Eagle. While most are groomed, some are left alone so people can explore the fresh snow. Check the grooming report online before you get to the mountain to see your options.

## Snowboarding

Solitude does have one small terrain park just off the Moonbeam Triple for people to explore their wild side. The jumps are small and the features are definitely for beginners. However, it is a nice size and a great way to learn.

Snowboarders are going to be a bit challenged by Solitude. Like Alta, the landscape is glacially formed and has tremendous steeps with large flat areas. While the resort welcomes snowboarders, they need to be prepared to pull off the board on occasion and do some walking.

The Summit Double has some great drops and the runs are wonderful for boarding. Also, the cruisers over on the Eagle Express Quad are great. However, if you opt to ride Honeycomb Canyon, you may end up walking a bit.

## Other Activities

Nordic skiers will be pleased to see that their needs have been considered as well. The Solitude Nordic Center provides 20km of cross-country trails with varying degrees of difficulty. The extensive trail system is focused on providing challenging runs in a setting that allows the skier to connect with nature.

If you are all about the alpine skiing, you can double your pleasure with the Solbright Connection. Brighton and Solitude resorts offer a combined lift ticket that will let you ski both resorts in a single day. The Solbright Trail will allow you to connect to Brighton and then back to Solitude very easily.

## Lodging

You can now enjoy the beauty of Solitude without having to leave the resort. Over the last several years, the resort has built a beautiful village reminiscent of European comfort. From the clock towers to the charming Bavarian design of the lodge, the character is charming and magical in the same instant.

As with everything at Solitude, you have all the options you might want. From hotel accommodations to town homes, your visit is tailored to your needs. They have also tied all of the lodging together with a program called Club Solitude. From the traditional soak in a hot tub to video games with your friends, Solitude helps you relax on and off the slope in a way that works for you.

## Restaurants

Solitude offers every choice imaginable for food with little effort to its visitor. From the hot dogs and burgers to five-star French dining, you choose. If you want something on the mountain and you want it fast, the Sunshine Grill is your ticket. It is located at mid-mountain between the Moonbeam Quad and Eagle Express Quad.

Sit-down service is only a short walk from the base. The Creekside Restaurant at the village has excellent food and service. If being waited on is too much for you, walk a little farther for some pizza and ice cream at the Stone Haus.

In all, Solitude goes beyond the basics and gives its visitor all the choices. You decide how much you want to ski, eat, and relax. They simply provide the service and options and let you enjoy it all.

## 12

# Sundance Ski Resort

## About the Resort

Art, nature, snow, cuisine, design, earth. Like a poem, Sundance pulls together many beautiful and different themes to tie it all collectively into a single impression. Visitors to this beautiful and special resort are able to not only exercise their bodies but their minds and souls as well. A visit to Sundance is pure poetry.

From the majestic Mount Timpanogos cradling the resort to the subtle Southwestern charm of its lodges, Sundance feels like it has always been a part of the landscape. And in some ways, it always has. With a winter sports heritage dating back to the 1940s, this picturesque location used to be known as Timphaven.

Of course, Sundance is often most known for its celebrity owner, Robert Redford. The environmental activist, artist, and star fell in love with the area while shooting the film *Jeremiah Johnson*. In an effort to preserve its natural beauty, Redford purchased the resort and 5,000 surrounding acres in 1969.

Redford has developed the resort into a teaching tool for an appreciation of the arts and the beauty of nature. As a promoter of independent and foreign cinema, the Sundance Institute is world renowned for its encouragement of creativity and inventiveness. Guests at the resort are treated to the Sundance Channel in their rooms and a screening theater on site.

RR3 Box A-1
Sundance, UT 84604

**Web:**
www.sundanceresort.com

**E-mail:** reservations@
sundance-utah.com

**Main:** 801-225-4107

**Snow Report:**
801-225-4100

**Ski and Snowboard
School:** 801-223-4140

**RESORT STATISTICS**

**Peak Elevation:** 8,250 feet
(2,514 meters)

**Base Elevation:** 6,100 feet
(1,860 meters)

**Vertical Drop:** 2,150 feet
(656 meters)

**Area:** 450 acres
(182 hectares)

**Night Skiing and
Snowboarding:** No

▲ A visit to Sundance is about returning to nature.

## ☺ Tips and Tricks

Everyone I spoke to said that the most common question is where is Robert Redford? While Mr. Redford and his family have a home at Sundance and do use its facilities, he is a very private person and is not in the habit of visiting with the guests.

Employees can't tell you where he lives, what he is doing, or whether he will be popping in for a visit.

Sundance also has strong environmental principles. Only 450 acres of the resort have been allocated for development. There is an enthusiastic recycling program and hybrid shuttle cars, and all the electricity at the resort is purchased wind power. They also have an on-site glassblowing facility that produces glassware for the resort using recycled materials.

Beyond all of this, Sundance is simply a delight to visit. It is a beautiful and engaging resort that strives to be different. Your visit is not simply about skiing and snowboarding. You can take an art class. There is a complete on-site spa. They host workshops and retreats. There is a gallery and some amazing restaurants.

Sundance creates more than a simple vacation. The resort stimulates your mind, body, and soul with activities designed to enrich and entertain. Skiing and other traditional activities are available as well. Yet, the true beauty of Sundance is its balance of recreation and inspiration. You will feel like you are living poetry in motion.

## About the Mountain

Sundance is arguably one of the most beautiful spots in Utah. The scenery surrounding the resort is spectacular. From its view of Mount Timpanogos to its rolling valleys and hills, the scenery is simply stunning. This alone helps make the Sundance experience wonderful.

Hidden up Provo Canyon, Sundance has served as the only ski resort on the south end of the Wasatch Front for years. Thus, you do get a lot of locals along with the destination skiers visiting the resort. This is great as many of the hosts and mountain service people have spent a lifetime enjoying Sundance and can provide great insight into the resort.

Sundance is not a large resort. In fact, it is rather diminutive when compared to its neighbors in Park City. However, the resort is an excellent place for beginner and intermediate skiers. The mountain is very manageable and provides more than enough terrain for everyone to enjoy.

The resort is really broken into two different mountains. Front Mountain is primarily intermediate and beginning runs and gives visitors a simple layout to find the skiing and snowboarding they desire. Back Mountain is all intermediate and expert skiing. Because of its smaller size, it is very easy to switch between the two areas.

Front Mountain has a single lift servicing the entire area. Ray's Quad does get a touch busy at the bottom but seems to handle visitors without issue. The lift is unique in that you can exit at three different points. There is a midway drop-off for beginners, a summit exit for people skiing Front Mountain, and an end exit bringing you to the base of Back Mountain.

Back Mountain is supported by two lifts. The Arrowhead Triple provides access to most of the back side and gives blue and black skiers a lot of choices from the summit of the resort. Experts are the only ones who will want to use the Flathead Triple, though there is intermediate access from the lift.

▲ Sundance isn't large but it has great terrain.

Surprisingly, there is a lot more to this mountain than what the trail map presents. The area does have a lot of skiing and snowboarding. While it is not considerable, it is more than enough mountain for most. In addition, it is a great compliment to the entire Sundance experience.

## ● Easiest Terrain

Sundance is a superb resort for new skiers and snowboarders. It is smaller in scale than many of the other resorts and the terrain is generally gentle. The more difficult terrain is not simply separated by a lift but an entire mountain. Green skiers and snowboarders will want to spend their day on Front Mountain.

## ☺ Tips and Tricks

Montoya is the run used by the ski school. If you want to avoid the crowds, you will need to avoid this run. Classes congregate just after getting off the midway point on the Ray's Quad and the area can see a lot of congestion.

If you are truly new to winter sports, Sundance provides a free tow rope at the base to help you find your balance. Once you get a little confidence, you can purchase a lift ticket and hang out on Ray's Quad for the remainder of your trip. Taking Ray's and getting off at the first of its three exit points will give you a comfortable ride down.

## ■ Intermediate Terrain

Terrain for intermediate skiers is spread across Sundance. In fact, skiers and snowboarders at this level will find most of the mountain accessible. Ray's Quad offers many nice choices. Intermediates should choose to ride to the summit to open up their options.

Take a ride to the top of the Arrowhead Triple to get the impressive views and to feel the entire vertical of the resort. This area is probably for intermediate riders who have some experience on their boards. There are some steeps and faster terrain. However, the runs are wide and well groomed.

## ☺ Tips and Tricks

Lone Pine is a really fun way to get over to Back Mountain. However, it is really flat when you start to head toward the Flathead Triple. Snowboarders will want to keep their speed or they will be pushing their way to the lift. The Flathead Triple is pretty much for experts only and should be avoided. There is a traverse to help you get out from the top, but if you just stay away, you won't really need to worry about getting caught in something above your ability.

## ◆ Advanced Terrain

Sundance is not without some challenging terrain. In fact, most of Back Mountain is dedicated to black diamond skiing and snowboarding. Even with a resort of this size, there are a lot of options from which to choose. Experts will definitely find runs that not only test their skills but are long and quite aggressive.

The Arrowhead and Flathead triples both serve a majority of the black skiing. However, Flathead is exclusively for experts. Its only fault is that the vertical ascent of the chair is not to the summit. If you really want to enjoy the backside of the mountain, you need to take the Arrowhead chair to the top.

### ◆ ◆ Experts Only Terrain

Located off the Arrowhead lift is the Far East, an area subject to avalanche control. You will need to check with the resort to see if access is permitted. It is a steep in-bounds region but has the feel of out of bounds. Ride the ridgeline and take a plunge into steeps and deep powder for a great adrenaline rush.

There isn't any other area of the mountain dedicated exclusively for double black skiing and snowboarding. However, for a resort of this size, it is amazing how much diversity and how many options are available for a visitor.

## Cruisers

On the Front Mountain, Maverick is a great escape from the crowds. It diverts around a lot of the traffic coming off Ray's. Flatnose is also a real blast and a fun cruiser that can give you speed. Both are off the normal routes that skiers and snowboarders use to descend to the base and should be fairly empty even on a busy day.

Round Up is a long catwalk lined with tall pines for those looking for an easier way from Back Mountain. It is a really fun jaunt, and while flat in places, the scenery is great. In addition, it is a long ride.

## Bumps

Those wanting to rock on the bumps will find a few treasures on Sundance. Even with its exposed face, the top of Bishop's Bowl has nicely formed bumps and great steeps. The Badlands and Junior's located off the Grizzly Ridge are also excellent mogul fields.

If you want a little shorter jaunt, ride over to Quick Draw or Hawkeye. Both have good protection from the wind, which means the snow stays on the run and makes the bumps a breeze. Intermediates wanting to pick up bump skiing can use these two runs to learn.

## Trees and Steeps

There are two notably steep runs underneath the Flathead Triple. Both are narrow and quite challenging. Redfinger and Drop Out have nice vertical. Drop Out is a bit more direct and bumpy. Redfinger is longer and a bit steeper. Both provide good vertical and quick turns.

Rumor has it that Redfinger earned its name when Robert Redford took some seriously rough turns on this one, struggling the entire time. At the bottom, a friend asked him what he thought of this difficult run and Mr. Redford used his red glove to express his feelings. Whether the story is true or not, it may give you the satisfaction of knowing you can handle the run better than its famous owner.

Sundance does not have an abundance of glade skiing. There are a few short jaunts over on Front Mountain, and of course, you can find period spots here and there. Experts seeking out the trees will have to consult the kids. Flat Nose is the only notable tree skiing at the resort and it's for the little people.

## Powder

Sundance gets its fair share of Utah's wonderful powder and it can be found mostly on Back Mountain where many runs are left ungroomed. Take Hill's Headwall over to Freddie's from the top of the Arrowhead Triple if you want to get into the fresh snow. These are popular spots because of their easy access.

After a daytime fresh snow, intermediates can get their powder legs over on Bear Claw or Wildflower. Both have a nice pitch for the deep snow and the altitude to boot. However, instead of bumps or steeps underneath, you will find smooth groomers. In fact, if the snow falls overnight, the snowcats may have already cleared those off.

For the more aggressive rider, a traverse over to Shauna's and Shauna's Secret have the steep to make the deep work right. Riders will need to be prepared for a fast descent into a great valley. Pipeline at the bottom is a great ride out. Still, you may want to cut over early and cut through the Badlands so you can get back to the summit on the Arrowhead Triple.

▲ Learn pottery, painting, or photography. Sundance is more than a ski resort.

▲ Many consider Sundance one of Utah's most beautiful settings.

## Snowboarding

Snowboarders will find that while the terrain at Sundance is well suited to the sport, there is nothing specially designed to accommodate their visit. At the current time, there are no half-pipes or terrain parks, but Sundance aims to please and there may something in the future.

## Other Activities

Nordic skiers will be pleased to know that they can also enjoy the beauty of Sundance. The resort provides 26km of groomed trails through the woods surrounding the resort. Rentals are available right at the resort and you can even get lessons. In addition, they also provide 10km of separate trails for snowshoeing.

◄ Snowboarders will find the wide open runs at Sundance fun for riding.

## ☺ Tips and Tricks

If you tire of skiing or being outdoors, make a trek over to the Art Center. Classes are offered in pottery, painting, jewelry making, and photography. It is an excellent diversion and unique to Sundance.

## Lodging

Sundance lodging is a collection of cabins and homes scattered across hills and valleys above the resort and nestled among towering pines and aspens. Each is unique and beautifully decorated in the trademark Southwestern style of Sundance.

▲ Sundance is artistic in every
sense. Every detail is covered.

While the theme may be rustic, every amenity has been considered. Rooms come equipped with kitchenettes, wireless Internet access, and DVD players. In addition, some very nice personal touches have been provided including a nice selection of books and wood fireplaces.

Because the lodging is very much part of what makes Sundance unique, visitors really should take the opportunity to stay at the resort. The distinctive design and layout of the resort is something that needs to be experienced. It is unlike any other resort you might visit.

## Restaurants

Sundance actually has many wonderful restaurants. However, they are hidden away from the base area in the resort complex. By the lift you will find the Creekside Grill, which is a small hot dog and chili spot. It gets very busy at lunch. However, if you ride to the top of the Arrowhead Triple you will find Bearclaw's Cabin.

### ☺ Tips and Tricks

The Creekside Grill at the base of the mountain is usually packed at lunch time. Its fare is nothing special though they do make good chili. Take a short walk over to the Deli or Foundry Grill for fewer crowds and wonderful food.

Bearclaw's is a great spot. Located at over 8,000 feet, the restaurant has incredible views. On a clear day, you can see Utah County and the northern resorts. The comfortable décor, warm fire, friendly service, good food, and great location make it a natural spot for you to drop in for a warm-up cup of cocoa or lunch.

## ☺ Tips and Tricks

The environmental sensibilities of the resort translate into more than just good energy use. Sundance actually makes the glassware they use from recycled glass. They use hybrid cars to transport you around the resort. They also allow you to recycle any materials you want to toss. So, before you throw that old newspaper in a garbage can, you may want to drop it at the Recycling Center.

## 13

# Wolf Mountain Resort

## About the Resort

Among the giants of Utah, Wolf Mountain seems dwarfed by comparison. Its three small lifts and limited terrain do not compare in dimension to the other resorts. It is not as high and it doesn't have a huge vertical drop. However, sometimes good things come in small packages.

Wolf Mountain does not try to be something it is not. It doesn't want to compete with the other resorts in the state in size or features. They understand what they are all about and strive to be the best. What they are is a great place to get introduced to skiing or snowboarding at a very affordable price.

No other Utah resort can offer skiing for four people at about the same price it would be to take them to a nice dinner. Wolf Mountain excels in providing great value in a small but very fun resort. Visitors will find everything they need in a convenient and easy package.

The key to Wolf's success is in the fact that they offer a wonderful PSIA (Professional Ski Instructors of America) certified ski school. This means you can get the same quality of instructor but at a smaller resort for a much better price.

### ☺ Tips and Tricks

The parking lot is amazing. Yes, you read that correctly. Every skier and snowboarder knows the burden of getting dressed and then having

3567 Nordic Valley Way
Eden, UT 84310

**Web:** www.wolfmountain
eden.com

**E-mail:** contact@wolf
mountaineden.com

**Main:** 801-745-3511

**Snow Report:**
801-745-3511

**Ski and Snowboard
School:** 801-745-3511

**RESORT STATISTICS**

**Peak Elevation:**
11,000 feet
(1,920 meters)

**Base Elevation:** 5,300 feet
(1,615 meters)

**Vertical Drop:** 1,000 feet
(305 meters)

**Area:** 110 acres
(45 hectares)

**Night Skiing and
Snowboarding:** Yes

▲ Wolf Mountain has excellent night skiing that is very accessible.

to haul your gear what seems to be miles up to the base. On the other hand, Wolf Mountain has walk-up skiing.

Simply pull your car up into the parking lot and walk on to the slopes. If you have kids and want to have them spend the day in lessons, you can drive up to the Ski School Yurt and drop them off.

Visitors to Utah looking for an uncomplicated beginning to their vacation should explore Wolf Mountain. The manageable size of their slopes, abundant night skiing, and friendly staff are what you should expect on a visit. Easy on the body and easy on the pocketbook, Wolf Mountain is the best place for skiers and snowboarders to get their start.

## About the Mountain

If you have never been on a pair of skis or a snowboard before, you may want to start your vacation at Wolf Mountain. The mountain is far smaller and much less daunting than its Utah counterparts. It sits at a lower altitude, which will help you acclimate. Last, it provides both day and night operations for the entire resort. You can show up anytime and begin to learn.

The resort is broken into a two distinct areas. The beginner area and terrain park sit at the bottom right of the mountain. The Howling Wolf Double services the remainder of the resort. These two areas only comprise a total of 110 acres. However, there is a lot more to this mountain.

## ☺ Tips and Tricks

The Wolfeedo Double is an easy access to the terrain park and many snowboarders will use this chair and cut in below the top. However, if the resort is very busy, they restrict access to the park from the top of Wolfeedo. This means you have to take the Howling Wolf Double and exit midway.

Just like a small local bookstore, your choices are limited, but if you look a bit you might find something to treasure. The mountain has many small but interesting features. There are some fun gullies, natural half-pipes, great drops, and wonderful cruisers. Even with short runs, you feel like you are getting more than you anticipated.

Wolf Mountain has lighting installed on the entire resort so you can pop in after work to make a few runs. They also have extensive state-of-the-art snowmaking equipment. The mountain is always ready and waiting no matter what your schedule.

The staff at Wolf Mountain also strives to provide the best grooming possible. They realize a lot of people are making their first turns ever on their slopes. The grooming staff spends extra time to make certain the snow is soft and even.

Finally, snowboarders will be in heaven. The terrain park at Wolf Mountain rivals those at the bigger resorts. The Wolf's Lair has close to 20 different features and three massive jumps. It is a fantastic place to work on your grinds or to master an ollie. Unlike the other resorts, it's a short lift to be able to ride over and over again.

## ● Easiest Terrain

When learning, everyone starts on the Wolfdeedo Double. This chair is served by two easy runs that have a very gentle pitch and bring you back safely to the bottom. Its only hitch is the occasional snowboarder who is using it for access to the terrain park. Just be patient and let the more advanced person ride off while you get ready.

Off the Howling Wolf Double, you can find one green run. The meandering Bayot's Boulevard gives you a nice long run to work on your form and improve your confidence. It has a nice slope but does get crossed a few times by more advanced runs. Keep your eyes open.

## ☺ Tips and Tricks

There is a midway stop on the Howling Wolf Double that will give you a nice easy run back over to the Wolfdeedo on Bayot's. In addition, it is a faster route for snowboarders looking to get to the top of the terrain park.

While crowds are not usually a problem at Wolf, the number of beginning skiers and snowboarders at the base of Wolfdeedo can start to grow if a few take a spill getting on the lift. Pop down to the Howling Wolf Double and use the midway exit to stick to greens.

## ■ Intermediate Terrain

If you are looking to hone your skills and move to the next level of skiing or snowboarding, you have picked the right place to do it. The layout of Wolf allows you to drop in and out of blue runs while sticking to greens for a good portion of the day. The short blue runs give you a taste of the next level without being too aggressive.

Solid blue skiers have this advantage as well. The superior mix of intermediate and expert terrain provides the perfect launch pad to go from good skier to expert. Drop in and out of the black runs all day while sticking primarily to blue.

## ◆ Advanced Terrain

Believe it or not, there are some challenging runs at Wolf. Nothing here will scare an expert, but there are some excellent steep spots, a couple natural half-pipes, and some fun bump runs. You may not leave the resort raving about the terrain you conquered, but it will certainly provide something to explore while the kids are in ski school.

Barney's Way is all about the vertical and you can get some thigh burning speed if you hit it from top to bottom. Cougar Canyon has some nice drops and bumps. However, make certain to watch for people when you cross Bayot's. Finally, Chainsaw Willy is a nice tight drop with some fun angles.

▲ Wolf Mountain provides close access to Ogden Valley's other resorts and activities.

## ◆ ◆ Experts Only Terrain

If you can find experts only terrain on this mountain, you have discovered something hidden. This resort is not about double blacks but about double your fun without beating up your pocketbook. Perhaps all you extreme skiers could use a break and take some relaxing time with your family at Wolf Mountain.

## Cruisers

Wandering Wolf has all the elements of a good cruiser. It is long and smooth and has just enough vertical to keep you going at a nice speed. It is what everyone looks for when they simply want to make some turns. The run merges with several other great blue runs, which extends your options and allows you to finish it nicely.

A bit shorter but just as sweet is Lobo Lane. It can be combined with Moose Run to get some more cruising, but it doesn't have as

▲ Sipping cocoa after a lesson is one of the great rewards of learning at Wolf Mountain.

many options as Wandering Wolf. Nevertheless, it is a fun cruiser that's nicely groomed and has a respectable length.

## Bumps

Bumps form where they form at Wolf Mountain. The limited number of expert skiers and the smaller terrain restrict the number of good bump runs. If you are looking to snag a few moguls, check out Dyer Straits or Ecker's Roll. However, the grooming and amount of snow will determine if these runs are simply steeps or they have some bump action.

## Trees and Steeps

The best steep shot is Barney's. You can build nice speed on this long, fast face. Also check Coyote Canyon and Dyer Straits for more vertical. All have a nice pitch and will certainly give you enough vertical.

Tree skiing and snowboarding can be found on Hawkins Hold and Chainsaw Willy. It is not a large area, but it may satiate that

**190**   Utah: The Complete Ski & Snowboard Guide

desire to hop into a glade and see the powder fly. The kids also seem to have fun making runs through the trees on the lower area over by Meadow Park.

## Powder

Wolf Mountain focuses on grooming, but after a dump they let the snow stay on some runs. They may groom half a run to ensure that the powder hounds and those wanting to learn to ski the powder both can enjoy the fresh snow.

In all, Wolf does get the powder and they do leave some but keep the focus on their mission as a learning resort. Check out Aspen Chute, Cougar Canyon, and the edges of Wandering Wolf to find some of the best fresh snow at the resort.

## Snowboarding

Snowboarders will find Wolf Mountain a welcome home at which to hone their shredding skills. The resort not only has some nice surface for carving the big turns and jumping, it also has a terrific terrain park. With jumps soaring 20, 30, and 40 feet, plus nearly 20 features, the Wolf's Lair will give any rider a great opportunity to play.

## ☺ Tips and Tricks

Moms and Dads dropping kids off at Wolf Mountain need to remember that if the kids are renting and are under 18, they can't sign the rental paperwork. In addition, if you rent your gear from a shop off the mountain, the resort can't help your kids fix a broken binding or adjust a foot plate.

## Other Activities

Those looking for something less vertical and more scenic may want to rent some cross-country gear or snowshoes and explore North Fork Park in Eden. Nearly 20km of trails have been groomed and maintained to give Nordic skiers a chance to get out into the woods. The scenic area is surrounded by mountains and is easily accessible from Wolf Mountain. Check out the web site at www.wolfcreek resort.com/North%20Fork%20Park%20Trails.pdf

## Lodging

Wolf Creek Resort is the owner of Wolf Mountain. However, Wolf Creek does not play favorites and supports all the Ogden Valley ski areas. Their condos and private homes provide some of the best lodging in the valley. In addition, they also have two great restaurants and all the amenities of a true winter resort.

The Ogden Valley also has a number of other options available if Wolf Creek is not an option. Bed and breakfasts and other condos can be found in Huntsville and Liberty, the other two valley communities. Ogden is also a short 40 minutes from the area and has many national hotel chains available.

## Restaurants

A refashioned barn serves as the chalet for Wolf Mountain. It holds

▲ Learning to ski or snowboard is great at the inexpensive and convenient Wolf Mountain.

the ticket office, rentals, and of course, a small cafeteria. The interior no longer has any connection to its roots. Instead of farm implements, the walls are decorated with old skis, poles, and posters from the sport's past.

The restaurant is a great place to warm up with a hot chocolate or coffee. They offer a nice selection and the prices are surprising reasonable. In all, the food is nothing more than simple ski fare, but the barn's quaint size and the staff's friendly service make it a great place to break any time of the day.

If you want to make the day at Wolf a touch fancier, the Wolf Creek Resort is a short drive from the mountain and has fine dining in its restaurant, The Grille. Filet mignon Oscar, lamb chops, or king salmon are only a few of the delights available. The restaurant features panoramic views of the valley and delicious food.

# Glossary

**Aerials**
The art of jumping and doing acrobatics on skis or a snowboard in the air.

**Alpine Skiing**
Another name for downhill skiing.

**Après Ski**
After-skiing activities usually involving hot tubs and beverages.

**Base**
The bottom of the resort where the lodge is located.

**Basket**
The small, plastic circular object at the bottom of a ski pole.

**Binding**
An apparatus used to attach a boot to a ski or snowboard.

**Black**
Most difficult. Used in reference to ski terrain. Usually the text of the name and a black diamond symbol are used to indicate this level of run.

**Blue**
More difficult. Used in reference to ski terrain. Usually the text of the name and a blue square symbol are used to indicate this level of run.

**Bomb**
Racing from top to bottom without stopping.

### Boundary
Signified by an orange sign or rope. Used to designate where avalanche control at a resort ends.

### Brakes
Device on bindings that prevents skis from sliding down the mountain.

### Bumps
Created by skiers and snowboarders continuously carving a specific path down the hill. Bumps are also called moguls.

### Carve
The act of using the edge of a ski or snowboard to turn on the snow. The edge carves a turn on the snow.

### Chute
A narrow path between two rock encampments.

### Concrete
Exceptionally hard-packed snow. Hard to ride and requires good edges.

### Corduroy
The snow created after the snowcats have groomed. Named for the appearance of the snow. Wonderful to ride.

### Corn
Hard, crumbly small bits of snow made from constant temperature shifts. Easy to ride and snowboard.

### Crud
Large chunks of hard snow that have formed and frozen making it hard to edge or push through.

### Crust
Soft snow underneath hard snow. Your weight pushes through the crust and the soft snow and breaks the crust. Very difficult to ride.

### Cross-country
Another name for Nordic skiing.

### Double Black
Experts only. Used in reference to ski terrain. Usually the text of the name and two black diamond symbols are used to indicate this level of run. In some cases yellow is also incorporated.

**Double Green**

Advanced beginner. Used in reference to ski terrain. Usually the text of the name and two green circle symbols are used to indicate this level of run.

**Downhill Ski**

Another term used for skiing. Alpine skiing is also used.

**Edge**

The thin metal strip along the side of a ski or snowboard. It is used to hold your position on ice and for turning.

**Express**

Term used to describe high-speed chairlifts. Express chairs detach and reattach to the cable to carry the chair to the top faster.

**Fall Line**

This is a straight downhill path made when descending down the mountain.

**Feature**

Elements of a terrain park. Features can be rails, tables, jumps, and other obstacles.

**First Tracks**

The act of carving fresh powder before another person.

**Glade**

A collection of trees cut specifically to allow skiers and snowboarders to ride through them.

**Glading**

The act of clearing trees for the purpose of creating healthy forest and for skiing and snowboarding.

**Gondola**

A chairlift with small cars holding up to eight people.

**Green**

Beginner. Used in reference to ski terrain. Usually the text of the name and a single green circle symbol is used to indicate this level of run.

**Groom**

The act of smoothing and softening slopes to make them easier to ski. Grooming is performed by snowcats after hours to improve conditions.

### Ice

Ice is a smooth hard surface that rarely occurs in Utah.

### Mashed Potatoes

The condition of snow when the weather gets warmer and makes the normally dry Utah powder softer and heavier.

### Moguls

Created by skiers and snowboarders continuously carving a specific path down the hill. Moguls are also called bumps.

### Nordic

Another name for cross-country skiing.

### Packed Powder

The condition of the snow after grooming.

### Piste

Another name for a ski run.

### Pitch

The measurement used to determine the angle of a slope.

### Poma

A small surface lift that features a disc on which people ride to get to the top.

### Powder

Utah's finest substance produced in abundance every winter.

### Powder Hound

Someone who loves the powder and seeks it out whenever possible.

### Powder Pig

Someone who loves the powder, seeks it out, and then won't go home until kicked off the mountain.

### Quad

Four-person chairlift.

### Rails

Terrain park feature that riders slide on with their edge.

### Rope Tow

Surface lift involving a rope that pulls you to the top.

### Ruts

Small surface hole on hard-packed snow that is created from excessive skiers. Rare in Utah.

## Shape Ski
Skis retaining an hourglass figure. This innovation has improved the ease of skiing.

## Skier's Left
Your left-hand side when you are skiing downhill.

## Skier's Right
Your right-hand side when you are skiing downhill.

## Slope
Another name for run.

## Slush
The condition of snow at the base of a mountain during spring skiing. Usually a bit sloppy and hard to ski on.

## Six-pack
Six-person chair lift.

## Snorkel
Common Utah occurrence when the powder is so deep you need a snorkel to breathe.

## Steep
Run with exceptional vertical.

## Tables
Terrain park feature that riders slide across with their flats.

## Telemark
Sport using skis and detachable boots. Popular with backcountry skiers.

## Terrain Park
Place to jump, ride, flip, shred, and crash.

## Touring
Another name for cross-country skiing.

## Tram
Ski lift with two separate cars that alternate from end to end while ascending and descending.

## Triple
Three-person chairlift.

## Tune
Service that typically adjusts bindings, waxes bottoms, and sharpens edges. Necessary for best performance of your equipment.

### Twin-tip
Skis with the same front and back. Used in terrain park.

### Uphill Ski
The ski that is on top when you are sideways to the hill.

### Wax
Compound placed on the bottom of a ski or snowboard to help improve speed and surface performance.

### Wedge
Pointing your two skis with the tails outward and the points together forming a triangle.

### Yard Sale
A crash of a skier or snowboarder when all their gear is thrown across the slope.